Communicating At Work

John W. Williams

Assistant Professor of Business Education
Oklahoma State University

Steven A. Eggland

Associate Professor
The Center for Vocational Teacher Education
The University of Nebraska-Lincoln

Published by

G19 SOUTH-WESTERN PUBLISHING CO.

CINCINNATI   WEST CHICAGO, ILL.   DALLAS   PELHAM MANOR, N.Y.   PALO ALTO, CALIF.

ISBN: 0-538-07190-7

Library of Congress Catalog Card Number: 77-88606

1 2 3 4 5 6 7 8 9 0 K 8 7 6 5 4 3 2 1 0 9

Printed in the United States of America

Preface

Effective communication may be the single most important part of modern work life. The work life may be in a restaurant, hospital, store, office, or factory. In all cases messages are sent to and received from employers, employees, customers, and fellow employees daily. This book will help students to communicate more effectively at work and in their personal lives as well.

This 1st edition of *Communicating at Work* is unique among communication text-workbooks. It is written specifically for the employee of the 1980s. Sophisticated principles of organizational behavior and more subtle forms of interpersonal communication are integrated and presented in everyday language and reinforced with concrete examples. Time-tested learning principles of variety and repetition are fully utilized to maximize comprehension. The use of jargon and technical terms has been avoided. The book is rich in photographs and illustrations to further aid students in understanding the written text.

This book is divided into six chapters which enable students to master the **communication competencies** required in an ever changing world of work, particularly in entry-level positions. We suggest that the teacher consult the *Teacher's Manual* for further information. Chapter 1 sets the stage for an enjoyable and stimulating experience by describing the wide scope of communication and stressing its vital importance at work. Chapter 2 focuses on communication *to* employers — an often overlooked area of communication. Chapter 3 is devoted to the many and varied forms of communication *from* employers. Communicating with customers, the most important segment of any free enterprise system, is discussed in Chapter 4. This chapter notes that whether customers are clients, purchasers, or patrons, effective communication is often the difference between profit and loss or success and failure. Chapter 5 discusses how a new employee or an experienced employee in a new job can best establish and maintain effective communication with fellow employees. Chapter 6 is designed to provide case-study capstone experiences which summarize and integrate the subject matter of the entire text.

At the end of each chapter are several "class activities" that, like the rest of the text, are appropriate for secondary and post-secondary students. These activities, as well as some exercises interwoven in the chapters, are designed to provide realistic, participative experiences that will help to develop the concepts brought out in the chapters. Because of the nature of organizational behavior and interpersonal communication, many of these activities involve group work and group interaction. The teacher is encouraged to be flexible and creative when directing the class activities. Suggestions for expanded and additional activities are found in the *Teacher's Manual*.

Finally, this text-workbook may be used in a great variety of settings and over varying lengths of time. It is appropriate in virtually any vocational education class. The text is written for students from ninth grade and up. The time consumed could range from six weeks to a full semester. It could be a part of another class or become a class in itself. Its use will depend on the professional teacher's analysis of students' needs.

It is often said that experience is the best teacher, but experience becomes meaningful only when one is ready to learn. It is the authors' sincere wish that this publication serve to enhance the learning opportunities of those who are in or who are about to enter the world of work.

J.W.W.
S.A.E.

1979

Contents

The Importance of Communicating at Work

Communicating with others is a vital part of modern work life. The work life may center around any office or work area in a business firm, restaurant, school, hospital, or even out in the open. In any case, messages must be sent to and received from employers, employees, customers, and fellow workers daily. This book will help you communicate more effectively at work and in your personal life as well.

This first chapter will help you understand why good communication is so important at work. Read it carefully and then complete the activities at the end of the chapter. If you do this, you will be able to answer the following questions:

- What is business communication?
- Why is communicating at work important?
- What is feedback?
- Is it possible to communicate without words?

WHAT IS BUSINESS COMMUNICATION?

Words are a very important part of our everyday lives. The first words of babies are usually remembered for a lifetime. People's last words are repeated with reverence. Our society produces more words than anything else. For example, millions of books are written and read every year. Newspapers and magazines are published by the hundred thousands every day. Radio and television carry verbal and pictorial messages over the airwaves 24 hours each day. Billboards describe new products, people send greeting cards, and grandparents telephone grandchildren. Friends share secrets and baseball players argue with umpires. In each case people are communicating, or are at least trying to communicate. Activity 2 on page 23 will help you understand the many ways in which people communicate.

ILLUS. 1-1 People communicate in many different ways

Most people know and use thousands of words. We learn our first words very early in life. We use them to communicate needs and moods to others. As we grow older, new words are added to our vocabulary. Eventually we are able to talk to almost anybody who speaks our language. But sometimes we use words or actions and really don't communicate. That is, we talk or write; but for some reason people don't understand what we are trying to say. Learning to communicate is really learning to understand and to be understood.

Everyone needs to be able to communicate effectively. To be understood by others when communicating is the most important part of a study of communications. It is safe to say that a large share of problems at work and in personal life are a result of inadequate communication. Activity 3 on page 24 will give you an idea of the importance of communicating at work.

A Definition of Business Communication

To help lay a foundation for your study of communicating at work, it will be helpful to develop a definition of business communication. Very simply, people are attempting to communicate when they are

ILLUS. 1-2

Two people *not* communicating

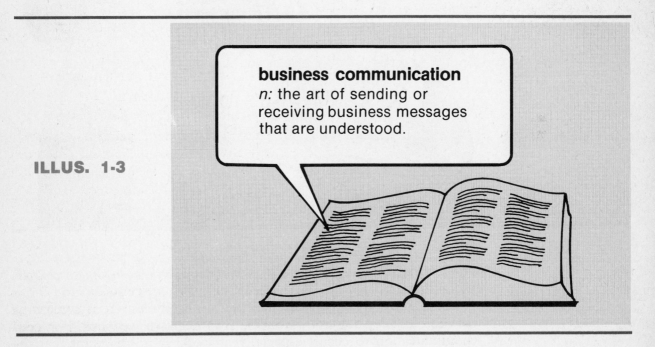

ILLUS. 1-3

business communication
n: the art of sending or receiving business messages that are understood.

sending and receiving messages. True communication has occurred when those messages are completely understood by the people who are sending and receiving. So, a good definition of business communication would be: **Business communication** is the art of sending or receiving business messages that are understood. Illustration 1-3 above should help you to remember this definition. Activity 4 on page 25 will help you put this definition of business communication into practice.

Providing Feedback

One of the most important words in the definition of business communication is "understood." A message is understood completely when the receiver provides feedback to the sender. For example, if you point to your empty coffee cup, the waiter is giving feedback when he says to you, "Would you like your cup refilled?" The waiter is really saying, "I see you pointing to your empty coffee cup and I assume you want more coffee. I wanted to make certain, so I asked you." Providing feedback is vital to effective communication.

ILLUS. 1-4

Portraying the definition of business communication, with a sender, a receiver, and a business message that is understood

It is possible for some kinds of feedback to be positive or negative. When the feedback message is something the receiver wants to hear, it is called **positive feedback**. When the feedback message is something the receiver may not enjoy hearing, it is **negative feedback**. For good communication to occur, especially at work, it is important that the feedback be honest and accurate whether it be positive or negative.

Positive Feedback

Suppose an employee asks the manager if a certain job was completed in a satisfactory manner. If the manager replies that the job was

ILLUS. 1-5

Providing feedback

ILLUS. 1-6

Positive feedback

very well done and the employee should be very proud, the employee would have received positive feedback.

People usually respond pleasantly to positive feedback. They like to hear that business is good, that their clothes are attractive, or that they are doing a good job. For example, Francine tries very hard to be pleasant and to say pleasant things around the office. One day, after she had paid a simple compliment to Jose, a fellow employee, Jose said, "Francine, that was a nice compliment. But even more important is the fact that you often say nice things to all of us. We really appreciate it and enjoy working with you because of it. We like working in this office with you." Francine experienced a good feeling! She received some unexpected positive feedback that made her feel very good. She smiled and thanked Jose for saying what he said.

Negative Feedback

At times feedback must be negative. For example, a store owner might ask a customer if the lawn mower he purchased recently was working all right. The customer might reply that the mower was of very poor quality and seemed to need repairs constantly. In this case the customer is giving the store owner negative feedback.

It is not pleasant to send or receive negative feedback. It is important, however, to be as honest and sincere as possible when sending negative feedback. When receiving negative feedback, you should work to be as understanding as possible.

One day Ms. Robinson approached David with this message: "I hope customer complaints have been reduced with our new billing

ILLUS. 1-7

Negative feedback

system." David knew that the billing system was still causing some problems with customers. He wanted to be honest and replied, "I'm afraid we are still getting quite a few complaints from customers on their bills." In order to make the required negative feedback a little easier to send and receive, he added, "But I think that as soon as we iron out some of the minor problems we have with the new system, it will be much better than the one we had before."

David felt that he must be honest with Ms. Robinson even though it meant giving negative feedback. In the long run, the business and the people involved will be better off if they are honest with one another. If David had replied that the new system was currently working well, that would have been a mistake.

Activity 5 on pages 26–27 will give you some experience in providing both positive and negative feedback to others.

WHY IS COMMUNICATING AT WORK IMPORTANT?

The easiest way to understand why communicating at work is important is to imagine a business in which there is no communication. Think of it! There would be no sign on the outside of the business. No one in the business would send or receive any mail. The people in the business — both employers and employees — would not talk with one another. There would be no telephones, no price tags, no conversations with customers, and no advertising. You can see that the business couldn't survive without the many forms of communication we have come to depend upon.

ILLUS. 1-8

Can you imagine a business with no communication?

Of course, communicating at work is important. It is vital to the success of *every* business.

In what ways must a business communicate or provide for communication? The answers can be arranged into four categories. It is important to:

1. Understand how to communicate *to* employers.
2. Receive and respond to communications *from* employers.
3. Know how to communicate with customers.
4. Know appropriate ways to communicate with fellow employees.

These four categories of communication are not all, however. There are several other groups of people with whom a business must communicate. Some people in the business will need to talk with deliverypersons, suppliers, buyers, salespersons, and meter readers. They will exchange messages with other businesses, city officials, politicians, and charitable group representatives. So, even though this book will concentrate on the first four categories of communication, you must remember that the list of situations in which good business communication is needed is almost endless.

Communications with an employer can be divided into two types: communications *to* an employer (a department head, boss, supervisor, owner, manager, etc.) and communications *from* an employer to you.

ILLUS. 1-9 A person at work must be able to communicate readily and effectively in at least four ways

Referring to Illustration 1-4 on page 4, you are the sender when communicating to your employer. When you receive communication from your employer, the employer is the sender and you are the receiver.

Communication to Employers

Your ability to communicate your thoughts effectively to your employer is important for two reasons. First, your employer *needs* ideas and information from you. Suppose you work for a business that sells goods. Your employer needs to know many things. For example:

1. Who are the best customers?
2. How effective is the advertising?
3. Which machines are providing good service, and which ones are frequently broken?
4. What makes the customers and the employees happy?

You can see that this list of reasons for communicating to employers can be endless. Activity 6 on page 27 will let you and your classmates add to this list.

The second reason why you should communicate well with your employer may sound a bit more selfish: It will help you to get more of what you want as an employee.

When you tell your employer what you like about working in the business, most likely your employer will remember what you have said. If you can describe your needs or your problems at work, most likely you will get results that will solve your problems. This is much better than suffering through a problem in silence. It is certainly better than

ILLUS. 1-10

Developing the ability to communicate with your employer will frequently be beneficial to you

complaining to people who cannot solve the problem such as customers, fellow employees, your friends, or your family.

Communication from Employers

It is equally important to develop skill in receiving communication from employers. In this case your employer is the sender and you are the receiver.

It is vital to the business that you understand exactly the communications that are directed to you from your supervisor. These communications will serve many purposes for the business. For example, you may be asked to order an item or call a customer. You may be asked to rearrange some desks or to advertise some merchandise. Whatever the reason for the communication, it is important to the business that you understand it. Much money and time is lost at work today because of inadequate communication. Improving the understanding of communications from employers can reduce these losses.

ILLUS. 1-11

Attention to communication from employers results in rewards for employees

Understanding directions, responding to suggestions, and paying attention to general communications from employers is also beneficial to the employee. All this results in improved employee performance. This improved performance, in turn, will be rewarded by promotions, pay raises, and recognition. Employers know who is paying attention to them and who is doing a good job for them, and they will provide appropriate rewards when these are due.

Communication with Customers

Customers of a business are among the most important groups with whom to develop good communications. "Without our customers," a retailer's motto goes, "we wouldn't be in business." And every businessperson knows that customers must buy goods or services from a business in order for it to make a profit. Communications with customers contribute to the health (profit or loss) of the business.

Communication between customers and employees usually centers around needs. If a businessperson can learn to understand what various types of customers need, communication will be improved. For example, customers need clothing, food, housing, and protection. They sometimes need ballet lessons, entertainment, or status symbols. It is important that these needs be communicated.

ILLUS. 1-12

Understanding a customer's needs is the first step to good business-customer communication

Many different goods or services are available to satisfy these various needs. Goods such as coats, cars, toys, or groceries satisfy some needs. Services like haircuts, movies, laundry, or insurance may satisfy other needs. Anyone spending for a good or service to satisfy a need is a customer. Understanding and satisfying customer needs is the main objective of a profit-making business.

Communication with Co-Workers

The last category, communication with co-workers, is also well-established as important. Learning to communicate well with your fellow workers is a skill that will give you great satisfaction and enjoyment. The difference is great between working in a place where co-workers communicate well and one in which they don't. As a customer, you can often sense this when you enter a place of business. Some businesses seem to hum with pleasantness. People talk amiably with one another. There seems to be no confusion. You see a lot of smiles and hear a lot of "Please's" and "Thank you's." In contrast, businesses where co-worker communication is poor seem cold, aloof, and boring.

ILLUS. 1-13

There is a noticeable difference between businesses with good and poor co-worker communications

As with the other types of communication at work, developing skill in communications with fellow employees will improve the business and make life more pleasant for the young businessperson. With good communication, fewer mistakes are bound to happen. Thus, customers will want to patronize that business. The employees in that business will be more productive, be absent from work less often, and be genuinely happier in their work. Good communication among fellow employees is truly a worthwhile goal.

Communicating at work in the four ways just described is treated in detail in Chapters 2 through 5 of this book. Chapters 2 and 3 deal with communication to and from employers. Chapter 4 discusses ways of improving several kinds of communication with customers. Chapter 5 will help you develop skill in communicating with co-workers. Finally, Chapter 6 will give you some experience in real-life situations where all kinds of communication skills are required.

ILLUS. 1-14

Working for the goal of good communication among fellow workers will provide many rewards

WHAT IS THE SCOPE OF BUSINESS COMMUNICATIONS?

You have so far been introduced to four settings in which business communication occurs. There is another way to classify communications. It arranges the scope of communications into the five categories of speaking, writing, reading, listening, and communicating without spoken words. Each of these categories can be used in each of the four settings of business communication described earlier in this chapter. For instance, you could *write* a message to an employer, a customer, or a co-worker. Or you could *speak* to a customer, a fellow employee, or your employer.

Good business communicators need to be skilled in reading, writing, speaking, listening, and understanding what people mean by their actions. Referring back to our definition of business communication, people need these skills when they send or receive messages.

Speaking

One of the first communication skills that we learn is speaking. We develop that skill as we grow older. Speaking is what many people think of when they think about communicating. Certainly speech is a very important method of communication, especially at work.

ILLUS. 1-15

Speaking is one of the first communication skills human beings learn

Businesspersons are called upon to send spoken messages in several ways and in several settings. They interview people for jobs and are interviewed for jobs. They talk to customers about merchandise and services. They often give directions or ask questions about directions. Most businesspersons must have skill in talking on the telephone.

Skill in talking is also required in other activities. Verbal deals are made with suppliers, and suggestions are made for the improvement of employee performance. Arrangements are made for days-off, and orders are requested from the stockroom — all with spoken words.

Although most of us are able to talk, we don't always communicate well. Sometimes the words we utter are poorly chosen and therefore not clearly understood. Frequently spoken messages are sent, but not received. Activity 7 on page 28 will give you some understanding of the problem of speaking but not communicating.

Listening

The topic of good listening as a communication skill follows naturally that of speaking. Each skill is enhanced by the other. The person receiving the spoken message is listening.

Unfortunately the skill of good listening in our society is not nearly so well developed as other communication skills. You have never heard of a "listening class," have you? There is no such thing as a listening contest. Nobody worries about your listening speed. For

ILLUS. 1-16

Businesspersons should be skilled in talking on the telephone

ILLUS. 1-17

Courses in listening are seldom offered

some reason everyone pays a lot of attention to speaking, reading, and writing but not much attention to listening.

Nonattention to listening doesn't make it any less important as a business communication skill; on the contrary. Because most people have little formal preparation, it is necessary that young businesspersons develop skill in listening. People at work must listen carefully to directions from employers, and they must listen to suggestions from co-workers and to messages on the intercom.

With each spoken message that is heard and understood goes the potential for a sale, a promotion, or a good feeling. With each message that is not heard comes the possibility of a mistake, a hurt feeling, frustration, or anger. Good listening skills, therefore, are important to good business.

Writing

Business writing is probably the most well-developed and best understood of the communication skills in business. Many courses and books are available for the improvement of business writing skills. This is proof that writing skills are needed by almost everyone who works in a business.

Business writing is most often illustrated in the business letter. Letters have been exchanged between businesspersons for centuries. The skill of business letter writing is now considered to be a highly developed art. You will have several opportunities to develop this skill while working with this book.

ILLUS. 1-18

Businesspersons have been writing and exchanging letters for centuries

In addition to letter writing, other writing skills are required at work. Memos, announcements, and directions are frequently written. And they must be well-written so as to be understood. Words for advertisements and invoices for goods and services rendered are always written. Applications for jobs and technical directions are also written. Several other examples of the requirements of business for writing skills could be given. But by now you should be convinced that business writing is an essential skill at work. Activity 8 on page 29 will help you develop your writing skills.

Reading

As one of the traditional "Three R's," reading has taken a prominent place in education. It has also assumed an important role in the preparation of people for business. Receiving written messages through reading is fast and efficient. Reading has the potential for being clear, concise, and easily understood.

Much reading is required of young employees in business.

Businesspersons read many different kinds of messages during a day. They read letters, of course. But they also read directions on boxes, memos from the boss, and notes on the company bulletin board. They spend some time reading company reports, signs on walls, and written complaints (or praise) from customers. All of this reading should be done rapidly and accurately. Making certain to receive the message the writer intended to send should be your goal for reading at work.

Communicating Without Words

Communicating without words is the most recent form of communication to receive attention. This form of communication has always been with us, but only recently have people begun to realize its importance. As you will see, some of the most significant communicating is done without using *any* words.

Communicating without using words may seem impossible when you first think about it. After all, if communication doesn't consist of words, what is it? Well, remember our definition. Communication consists of *messages* sent and received. After a couple of examples, you will soon understand what is meant by sending and receiving messages without words.

ILLUS. 1-19

How can people communicate without using words?

Trini was at the wheel of a car stopped at a red traffic light. He was adjusting the car radio when the light turned green. He didn't see this, and after a few seconds the driver in the car behind him began to blow her horn. No words were exchanged, but it was clear to Trini that the horn blast meant, "Get moving!" or "The light is green. Go!"

ILLUS. 1-20

People *can* communicate without words

Franco had been working very hard all day at typing medical reports for his supervisor. Shortly before it was time to leave work, he proofread the last report and took it out of the typewriter. Franco stapled the reports together and carried them to his supervisor's office. He handed the reports to her; she smiled and held up her hand, making a circle with her thumb and forefinger. She used no words, but her message was clear. She meant to communicate something like, "Thanks, I appreciate the fact that you have finished the job," or "Nice work, you are a good employee."

There are several other examples of nonverbal communication in business settings. Handshaking, waving, shoulder shrugging, and frowning are all forms of nonverbal communication. It is important to be able to send *and* receive nonverbal messages. Activity 9 at the bottom of page 29 will give you some enjoyable practice in using this form of communication.

ILLUS. 1-21 Most communication without words is easy to understand

SUMMARY

You are, by now, aware of the importance of communicating at work. You have read about four settings in which communication occurs. Five different forms of communication skills have been described. As you proceed through the remainder of this book, you will have many opportunities to experience these forms of communication in several combinations. They are designed to create awareness, to develop skill, and to motivate you to form a commitment toward improving communications at work.

CLASS ACTIVITIES
Instant Replay

This activity is titled "Instant Replay" because you have a chance to replay ideas from your reading assignment. Write a short answer to each of the questions below. As you replay the answers in class, remember that you are getting feedback on your understanding of the chapter.

Questions

1. Why are words important? List three examples to help explain your answer.

   _____

   _____

   _____

   _____

2. What is the meaning of the statement, "Learning to communicate is really learning to understand and to be understood"?

   _____

   _____

   _____

3. When does true communication occur?

   _____

   _____

4. Define and give an example of positive feedback.

   _____

   _____

   _____

5. Define and give an example of negative feedback.

_____

_____

_____

6. Which is more important, positive or negative feedback? Why?

_____

_____

_____

7. In what ways will communicating with your employer help you to be an effective employee?

_____

_____

_____

8. What is the first step in developing good communication between a business and its customers?

_____

_____

9. Why is it that little attention is given to listening skills?

_____

_____

10. Which of the communication skills is the most well-developed? Does this mean it is an area which we need not study?

_____

_____

11. How do people communicate without words?

_____

_____

_____

Name _____   Date _____

Understanding Different Ways of Communicating

This activity will help you understand that there are many ways to communicate something to someone. For instance, if you were an employer and wanted to communicate disapproval to an employee, you could:

1. Say, "I don't like what you did."
2. Frown at the employee.
3. Shake your finger at the employee.
4. Withhold the employee's next pay raise.
5. Send the employee a note indicating disapproval.

There are probably several other ways to indicate disapproval.

On the other hand, there are many ways you could communicate to someone that he or she is doing a good job. In the space below write down as many ways as you can that you could communicate approval to an employee.

_____

_____

_____

_____

_____

_____

_____

_____

_____

Importance of Effective Communication

Communication at work that is *understood* is very important. The case problem in this activity will help you to realize this.

Helen Carpenter was an employee of Jones Super Service gasoline station. One of her duties was to wash customers' cars. Ms. Harlow was one of Helen's regular customers.

Ms. Harlow came to the station on a Friday and said, "I plan to sell my car on Monday and I want you to fix it up nicely over the weekend." Helen assumed that Ms. Harlow meant she should wash it as she had done before. Helen immediately washed the car and parked it until Monday.

When Ms. Harlow arrived on Monday to pick up her car, she was angry. She said, "When I asked you to fix it up nicely, I meant that you should paint over the scratches, clean the engine, and wax the car. You have done none of those things." An argument developed. It ended when Ms. Harlow said that she would never return to Jones Super Service again.

Questions

1. What seemed to be the problem? _____

_____

_____

2. How would better communication have avoided the problem?

_____

_____

_____

_____

Name _____   Date _____

Identifying Senders and Receivers of Messages

You know that in effective business communication there is always a sender, a receiver, and a message that is understood. Listed below are several examples of business communication. Read the examples, then identify the sender and receiver. To help you get started, the first example has been completed for you.

1. An employer shakes hands with John, saying "Congratulations."

   Sender _____ **employer** _____

   Receiver _____ **John** _____

2. A customer receives a postcard from Winkles Department Store announcing a sale.

   Sender _____

   Receiver _____

3. Becky reads an advertisement for Dairly Ice Cream in the *Evening Star*.

   Sender _____

   Receiver _____

4. Florence tells Arlo that he can wait on the next customer who comes into the store.

   Sender _____

   Receiver _____

5. There is a sign in the restaurant that says, "We appreciate it when our customers refrain from smoking — The Management."

   Sender _____

   Receiver _____

Providing Positive and Negative Feedback

To provide you with experience in giving positive feedback and to show that you understand the concepts of positive and negative feedback, complete the exercises below. You should make up a positive feedback response and a negative feedback response for each statement that is given. The first statement has been completed for you to help you get started.

Statement #1: Well, Francis, how are sales this month?

Positive Feedback: **Sales are better this month than in any month in our history.**

Negative Feedback: **Sales are down from last month by 500 units.**

Statement #2: How do you like the way we have arranged the office?

Positive Feedback: _____

_____

Negative Feedback: _____

_____

Statement #3: The new security system should solve our shoplifting problems.

Positive Feedback: _____

_____

Negative Feedback: _____

_____

Name _____   Date _____

Statement #4: I hope you enjoy working for us as much as we enjoy having you work here.

Positive Feedback: _____

_____

Negative Feedback: _____

_____

Reasons for Communicating to Employers

   On page 9 you read about two reasons why it is important to communicate to an employer. Now be as thoughtful and creative as you can and see how many additional reasons you can develop as to why communicating *to* an employer is important *to the employer*. Write your reasons in the space below.

Developing Skills in Speaking and Listening

This activity will help you practice your listening and speaking skills. First, pick someone in the class you would like to know more about. Then take five minutes of class time to interview that person. Use the questions below to help you, and add questions to the list as you wish.

After all members of the class have completed their interviews, each person will introduce to the class the individual he or she interviewed. During your time to introduce the person you interviewed, remember that you are practicing your speaking skills. Be sure to speak clearly and with enthusiasm.

Questions

1. Where are you from? Where do you presently live?
2. What are your major areas of study? (Business, home economics, industrial arts, etc.)
3. Are you currently employed? What is the nature of your job and where do you work?
4. What do you do when you're not working or studying? (Hobbies, recreation, etc.)
5. What do you hope to be doing five years from now?
6. What is the most meaningful thing that has happened to you in the past year?

Developing Writing Skills

Write a letter of recommendation for a friend — YOU! Assume that you are very close to getting a super job. All that remains is to have a good recommendation written about you. Normally you ask someone who knows you very well and likes you very much to write the letter. In this activity assume that you are the person who knows you very well.

Be sure to write about your past successes and any good things you have done. Whenever possible, give an example of something your "friend" did which you believe will help get that special job. Then give the letter to your teacher.

Nonverbal Communication — Charades

Sending and receiving messages without using words is an important part of communicating at work. This activity will increase your understanding of nonverbal communication and give you practice with it.

Play any of the following categories for charades:

1. Movie titles
2. Song titles
3. Names of music groups
4. TV show titles
5. Best-seller book titles

When you are finished, your teacher will conduct a post-game discussion on the different nonverbal behaviors shown during the charade.

Communicating to Employers

Communication with employers may be divided into two parts: communication TO employers and communication FROM employers. Communication to employers is commonly called "upward communication." Communication from employers is referred to as "downward communication."

This chapter focuses on upward communication. The next chapter discusses downward communication. Read this chapter carefully, then complete the activities at the end of the chapter. By reading this chapter you will find answers to these questions:

- What is upward communication?
- What kinds of messages are communicated upward?
- Why do some employees conceal information from employers?
- How does information overload affect upward communication?
- Is effective upward communication possible?

DEFINITION OF UPWARD COMMUNICATION

When an employee communicates to an employer (or manager), the process is called **upward communication**. The term "upward" is used because managers have authority over employees. **Authority** means the manager has the power to give orders to the employees. In business you communicate upward to anyone who has authority over you. The upward flow of communication can be seen in the partial organization chart shown at the top of page 32. The salespersons are at the bottom of the chart, Level 1. When they communicate with the department manager, they communicate upward to Level 2. Sometimes

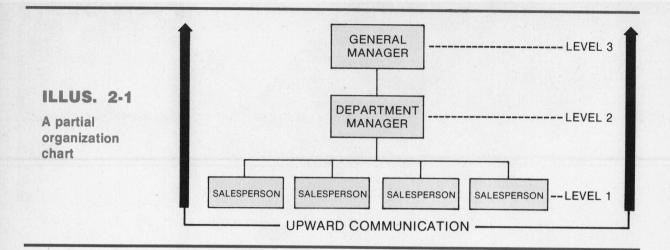

ILLUS. 2-1

A partial
organization
chart

GENERAL MANAGER — — — — — — — — — — — LEVEL 3

DEPARTMENT MANAGER — — — — — — — — — — — LEVEL 2

SALESPERSON SALESPERSON SALESPERSON SALESPERSON — LEVEL 1

UPWARD COMMUNICATION

they will communicate directly to the general manager. In this instance the communication flows from Level 1 up to Level 3. The department manager also communicates upward. When he or she communicates with the general manager, the communication is upward. In this case the communication flows from Level 2 to Level 3.

PURPOSE OF UPWARD COMMUNICATION

Keeping management informed about all aspects of the business is the main purpose of upward communication. As you learned in

ILLUS. 2-2

Managers need
both positive
and negative
feedback

Chapter 1, the process of keeping managers informed is called giving feedback. Without both positive and negative feedback, managers are cut off from information about the business.

When Managers Need Negative Feedback

Costly mistakes may occur when the necessary feedback is not provided. For example, Fred Jones, the manager of the men's clothing department of a large store, had planned a large sale of men's suits. A special shipment of men's suits was due at the store on Thursday for the sale scheduled on Saturday. The shipping and receiving clerks were expecting this special shipment. However, when the suits did not arrive on Thursday, the clerks failed to report it to the manager. Early Saturday morning Mr. Jones discovered that the special shipment of suits had not arrived, but it was too late to cancel the scheduled sale. The newspaper ads were already printed, so Mr. Jones decided to put a group of suits that were already in the store on sale.

What negative feedback should Mr. Jones have received from the employees? Write your answer in the space below.

Negative feedback: _____

_____

When Managers Need Positive Feedback

The Saturday suit sale mentioned on the previous page was a big success and, of course, Mr. Jones was very happy. On Saturday evening at closing time, he remarked to one of the salespeople, "I'm glad we had those other suits to put on sale. They really sold well." The salesperson said, "No wonder they sold well. That group of suits had already been selling fast earlier this week!" Naturally Mr. Jones became very upset because he realized that he had made a big mistake. The suits he put on sale should *not* have been on sale since they would have sold just as well at the regular price.

What positive feedback should Mr. Jones have received from the employees? Write your answer in the space below.

Positive feedback: _____

_____

All mistakes committed in this example cost the store a considerable amount of money. The employees made a mistake because they did not provide Mr. Jones with negative feedback — *that the special shipment of suits did not arrive on Thursday*. They also made a mistake when they did not give Mr. Jones positive feedback — *that the other group of suits was selling very well before the sale*.

TYPES OF UPWARD COMMUNICATION

Five types of messages are communicated upward. These messages may be either positive or negative. They are: (1) progress reports on assigned duties, (2) requests for help in solving problems and making decisions, (3) suggestions for improving the business, (4) routine requests for vacations and work schedule changes, and (5) feelings about the business.

The first four types of messages given above deal with work-related duties. The fifth type of upward communication deals with employee feelings about the work, the manager, and the business. This is the most troublesome area of upward communication. Before we study about this difficult area, let us first examine the four work-related types of upward communication.

Progress Reports on Assigned Duties

A **progress report** is a description of work completed or to be completed. This report is usually given in writing to a manager. Sometimes progress reports are given orally. This means that the employee tells the manager how a particular job is progressing.

The First Citizens Bank is seeking better ways to serve its customers. Sam, a teller at the drive-up window of the bank, has been asked by his supervisor to keep accurate records of the number of customers he

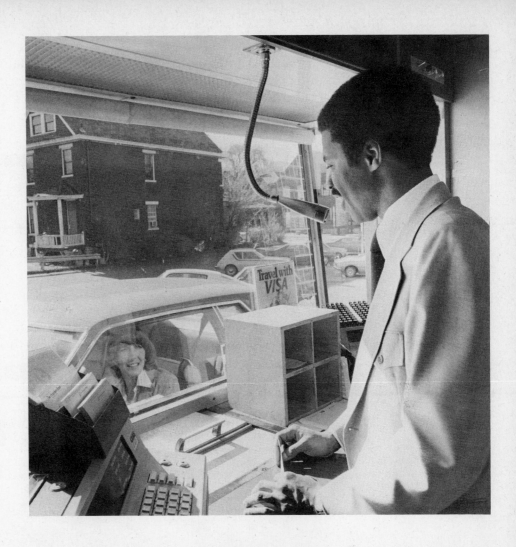

serves between 4:00 p.m. and 6:00 p.m. This time period is called the "rush hour." Sam has also been instructed to record the number of deposits to and withdrawals from checking and savings accounts, the number of checks he cashes, and the number of loan payments he receives. Illustration 2-3 below shows part of the progress report Sam is preparing. Sam's report will help the supervisor make a decision on whether or not more drive-up window tellers should be hired.

ILLUS. 2-3

Sam's written progress report

	CHECKING		SAVINGS		CHECKS CASHED	LOAN PAYMENTS
	DEPOSIT	WITHDRAWAL	DEPOSIT	WITHDRAWAL		
1						
2						
3						
4						

Betty, a delivery driver for American Parcel Company, also makes progress reports. Every person to whom Betty delivers a package must sign for it. The report includes the date, time, location, and size of the package delivered. It also bears the signature of each person who accepted a package from Betty.

The daily progress report Betty keeps is a legal record showing proof of delivery of packages. The report also tells Betty's supervisor how hard Betty works.

Requests for Help in Solving Problems and Making Decisions

Another form of work-related upward communication is a request for help in solving problems and making decisions. Both experienced and new employees ask their supervisors for such help at one time or another.

Billie Jo, a newly hired employee, works part time after school as a file clerk. Billie Jo was really eager to get this job at the Grant Insurance Agency because she wanted some work experience in an office during her senior year in school. She also wanted to earn some extra money to help pay some of the family's bills. Since this is the first job

ILLUS. 2-4

Billie Jo, a newly
hired employee

she has ever held, Billie Jo is having trouble in deciding which duties she should take care of first. She wants to finish her work on time so that she will make a good impression, but she is not sure how long a particular task will take. Billie Jo's supervisor simply showed her a stack of things to file and a pile of mail to sort. Her supervisor did not offer additional instructions.

To complete her job properly, Billie Jo must ask for more instructions. Her request to the supervisor for help in solving her problems is a form of work-related upward communication.

Suggestions for Improving the Business

A third type of work-related upward communication deals with offering suggestions for improving the business to the manager. Many businesses actively encourage their employees to make suggestions. To help promote suggestions, some businesses have a suggestion box system. A suggestion box is like a company mailbox. Employees simply write out their suggestion and drop it in the box.

A large number of companies offer cash bonuses to their employees for suggestions which improve either the products or services that the business offers. Even the federal government has a cash bonus system for employee suggestions.

Little ideas can result in big profits to businesses and employees. For example, automobile turn signals, the light in your refrigerator, and the ballpoint pen you write with started out as "little" ideas of employees. Of course, not all employee suggestions turn into profits; but many ideas can make a job easier. When you have a suggestion for improving the business, consider telling your employer about it. Your employer needs your suggestions.

Routine Requests

"Routine" means typical, common, or habitual. Thus, a routine request is one that is made many times by various employees. For example, when an employee wants to take a week's vacation, it is necessary to ask the employer. In high school a routine student request might be a pass to one's locker during class time. Other routine requests made by employees could include the following:

1. Time off to go to the doctor or dentist.
2. Changing break times with another employee.
3. Permission to have a friend or relative visit you while you are working.
4. Permission to use certain kinds of equipment.

Can you add other routine requests to the list?

5. _____

6. _____

Feelings About the Business

Employee feelings about the work, the manager, and the business are rarely communicated upward. Such feelings are often shared with co-workers, but they are generally not shared with management. The kinds of feelings to which we refer are listed in Table 2-1 on page 39.

Fear is the main reason why employees do not communicate feelings upward. Many employees believe that if they reveal their feelings, they will be penalized, embarrassed, or labeled as emotional. This barrier of fear, as well as other barriers to effective upward communication, are discussed in the next section of this chapter.

BARRIERS TO EFFECTIVE UPWARD COMMUNICATION

Many managers blame employees for ineffective upward communication. Such managers claim that the employees simply do not keep management informed. Similarly, many employees blame managers for the lack of good upward communication. Such employees say that managers won't listen to them.

Both managers and employees are half right and half wrong. Some employees do withhold information from their supervisors, and some managers simply do not listen to employees. Neither the employees nor the managers are to blame. The barriers to upward communication are largely human problems. Employees are human, as are managers. Problems or breakdowns in communication are bound to happen.

Feelings About Work	Feelings About the Manager	Feelings About the Business
1. Is the work load distributed fairly?	1. Does the manager tell employees when they do a good job?	1. Do the employees have a chance for promotion?
2. Are the working hours reasonable?	2. Is the manager interested in the personal life (hobbies, school, family) of the employees?	2. Are company policies fair?
3. Are the tools or equipment efficient and safe?		3. Are the employees proud of the business's reputation?
4. Is the furniture comfortable?	3. Does the manager have favorites?	4. Are the employees satisfied with company benefits (insurance, vacation time, sick leave)?
5. Is it clear as to who is to do what?	4. Are the employees supervised enough, too little, or too much?	
6. Are raises given to those who deserve them, and are the raises fair?	5. Are employees' complaints handled quickly and fairly?	5. Are the employees' lounge and restrooms adequate?
	6. Does the manager ask for the employees' opinions?	6. Are the employees informed about major changes in advance?

TABLE 2-1

Feelings that need to be communicated upward

Source: Adapted from the classic work of Earl Planty and William Machever, "Upward Communication: A Project in Executive Development." A more detailed presentation appears in *Personnel*, January, 1952, published by the American Management Association, Inc., New York.

The three major barriers to effective upward communication are: (1) fear of the manager, (2) information overload, and (3) the negative influence of other people.

Fear of the Manager

When employees give positive feedback, fear of the manager is *not* a problem. Employees enjoy giving managers pleasant reports, and managers certainly like to hear good news. For example, telling your boss that you made your daily sales quota makes both of you feel good. Describing to your boss how you helped a customer solve a problem is fun. Or telling your boss that you found a missing report he or she was looking for gives both of you pleasure. The point here is simple: *giving positive feedback to managers is not a problem*.

Giving Negative Feedback

Negative feedback includes all types of communication that you believe a manager may not like to hear.

Before reading further, try classifying the items on page 40 as positive or negative. Place a check mark ($\sqrt{}$) in the proper column.

ILLUS. 2-5

Giving negative feedback is difficult

Item	Positive	Negative
1. Telling your boss you are ahead of schedule.	_____	_____
2. Telling your boss you like working at the store.	_____	_____
3. Making your daily sales quota.	_____	_____
4. Asking your boss to repeat instructions.	_____	_____
5. Disagreeing with your boss.	_____	_____
6. Telling your boss a decision is unfair.	_____	_____
7. Being unable to work because of illness.	_____	_____

Now compare your answers with others in your class. Did you agree with everyone? Can you explain why you disagreed with some people in your class?

Employees do not like to give negative feedback to employers for many reasons. Some employees are simply nervous and shy around their boss. As a result, such employees do not talk to their boss very much. But even employees who are not shy have upward communication problems. The most serious upward communication problems center on describing negative feelings to employers.

Distorting and Concealing Negative Feelings

Most people try to avoid expressing negative feelings. But when we are angry or upset, we seldom avoid saying negative things. But generally people find it difficult to communicate negative feelings. To avoid giving negative feedback, we conceal and distort our true feelings.

Concealing means hiding, and **distorting** is the process of changing the appearance of something. For example, suppose you are about to go on a date and your date asks for your opinion of his or her clothes: "How do I look?" If you really do not like what your date is wearing, what do you say? Chances are you try to say something positive such as: "Say, those are definitely your colors!" This approach allows you to avoid giving your date negative feedback. By not directly answering the question, you conceal (hide) your true negative feelings. By telling your date that the colors are well chosen, you distort the truth.

ILLUS. 2-6

Distorting facts is a typical way to avoid giving negative feedback

We conceal and distort our feelings at times like this for two reasons. The first reason relates to our feelings. It is easier for us to say something positive than it is to say something negative. This way we spare ourselves the pain of dealing with a possible negative reaction from the other person. The second reason relates to the feelings of the other person. We assume that the other person would be upset by our true feelings. Therefore, to spare that person a bad feeling, we simply do not tell the whole truth.

In business the process of giving upward negative feedback is not easy either. It is hard enough to tell a friend your negative feelings, but it is even more difficult to speak about your negative feelings to your supervisor. For example, if the following things were true about you, could you tell your boss how you feel?

1. You resent having to work over-time on Saturdays.
2. You are never asked about the work schedule and you don't like it.
3. You dislike having to do work you were not hired to do.
4. Your boss makes fun of your lack of experience.

ILLUS. 2-7

Why Employees Distort and Conceal Negative Feelings

Negative feelings are difficult to express to an employer for many reasons. The three most common reasons are: (1) fear of being penalized, (2) fear of being embarrassed, and (3) fear of being labeled as emotional or weak. To avoid these fears, employees distort and conceal their true negative feelings.

Fear of Being Penalized. Alfonse, an ambitious young man, works at Chief Burger, a fast-food business. Alfonse wants very much to be promoted from assistant manager to manager. Last month the owner of Chief Burger, Mrs. Tangredi, met with Alfonse. They had discussed Alfonse's past performance and future goals. At that time Mrs. Tangredi told Alfonse that he and Alice, the night manager, were next in line for the job of day manager. Naturally Alfonse was pleased. Mrs. Tangredi then gave Alfonse a 15-cent-per-hour raise.

Alfonse was quite upset by the small raise. He believed that the raise should have been at least 25 cents per hour more, and actually he had expected a raise of 30 cents per hour. There was no question in his mind that the raise he received was unfair, but Alfonse did not express his true feelings to Mrs. Tangredi. He simply smiled, thanked her, and went back to work. Alfonse did not express his true feelings because he was afraid that complaining about the small raise would hurt his chances of being promoted to manager.

Many employees are like Alfonse. They are ambitious and want to be promoted. These employees will not reveal their true negative feelings to their boss. Employees like Alfonse believe that disclosing negative feelings might lead to punishment. The punishment, as in the case of Alfonse, would be to lose the chance of promotion.

Fear of Embarrassment. Employees will conceal and distort negative feelings if disclosure might cause embarrassment. The major danger of embarrassment comes from disagreeing with one's employer.

Carla's situation is a good example. Almost every day Carla disagrees with her employer, but she never voices her true feelings. Carla is the boss of a crew of shelf stockers at a large grocery store. The store manager, Ms. Santos, asks Carla and her crew to set up special displays of food products. Usually Ms. Santos asks Carla what she thinks about the location of the special displays. Before Carla answers Ms. Santos, she tries to figure out what Ms. Santos "wants to hear." For example, if Ms. Santos is excited about a display and tells Carla where to set it up, Carla usually agrees by saying, "Yes, that's a good location." At other times Ms. Santos will say, "Carla, do you think the display would be better here or over in Aisle 6? I kind of think Aisle 6 would be the best location." And Carla responds, "I think Aisle 6 is a good location."

ILLUS. 2-8

Carla does not disagree because she thinks she will be embarrassed

Sometimes Carla would like to disagree openly with Ms. Santos. However, she is afraid and does not know how to do it. Carla thinks that if she disagrees, Ms. Santos will get mad at her. Carla cannot forget that one incident in the past, when Ms. Santos corrected her in front of her crew. Carla had mistakenly set up a display of HITS ketchup when the manager wanted a display of DEL REY ketchup. When Carla said, "I thought you asked me to display HITS," Ms. Santos got angry and scolded her in front of her crew. This incident really embarrassed Carla. Since then, she has not openly disagreed with Ms. Santos.

Carla's refusal to give negative feedback to the manager hurts the grocery store. Carla knows the proper locations for certain displays, but she withholds the information. As a result, sales go down. Because of fear of being embarrassed, Carla chooses to conceal her true feelings about the display locations from Ms. Santos. What do you think Carla should do the next time she is asked for her opinion? Write your answer in the space below.

_____

_____

_____

Fear of Being Labeled as Emotional. Some employees believe that emotions or feelings should not be revealed at work. Such people often fear being labeled as emotional or weak.

Kurt works for Sound, Inc., a record shop. His work hours are from 9:00 a.m. to 5:00 p.m., Monday through Friday. Sound, Inc., is located in a shopping center and is open from 9:00 a.m. to 9:00 p.m., Monday through Saturday. The tapes and records sell very well. Business is so good that the shelves frequently need to be restocked with records and tapes.

Kurt's boss, Antonio Carreon, often asks Kurt to work overtime to restock the shelves. Most of the time Kurt does so when Mr. Carreon asks, but Kurt does not like to work overtime as much as Mr. Carreon asks. One day Kurt told his boss that he really preferred not to work overtime. Mr. Carreon replied, "Oh, come on, Kurt, a little work never hurt anyone. If you would stop whining about work, you would get a little more work done around here." Since that time, Kurt began to distort his true negative feelings. Now he has a string of excuses for not working overtime. Each excuse illustrates how Kurt distorts and conceals his true feelings. Some of his excuses are:

1. I'd really like to work tonight, Mr. Carreon, *but* I've got to take my sister . . .
2. Thanks for the opportunity to make some extra money, Mr. Carreon, *but* I have a date . . .
3. Gosh, Mr. Carreon, I know how badly we need to restock the shelves tonight, *but* I promised my mother . . .

4. Oh, I'd be happy to work overtime tonight, Mr. Carreon, *but* we have a guest from out of town and . . .

Kurt is unable to describe his true feelings to Mr. Carreon. He thinks that if he tells Mr. Carreon the truth, he will be labeled as being emotional or weak.

Information Overload

The second of the three major barriers to effective upward communication is called **information overload**. This means that the employer has more incoming and outgoing communication than any one person can manage.

When managers become overloaded with information, a communication breakdown occurs. In some ways an overloaded manager is like an overloaded electrical plug. What would happen if you tried to operate a toaster, a coffee pot, a refrigerator, an electric fan, and a lamp from the same plug? You would probably blow a fuse, resulting in a loss of electrical power.

Information overload is a problem for both managers and employees. Managers have a very difficult time doing their jobs, and employees find it hard to communicate with a manager who is too busy.

Dennis Moore is the owner of Moore Parts Company. He is experiencing information overload and, as a result, his employees are having upward communication problems. Serious communication breakdowns are about to happen. For example, today Mr. Moore is in an important meeting. The purpose of the meeting is to discuss the company's federal income tax problems. A concerned Mr. Moore is talking with two accountants when the phone rings. It's Doris, the credit manager. Doris needs an important decision from Mr. Moore. The Ace Company wants to buy $100,000 worth of parts on credit, but the standard credit limit is $50,000 in any one month. The large amount of money involved worries Mr. Moore, but he approves the transaction.

ILLUS. 2-9

Information overload

Mr. Moore returns to the discussion with the accountants, but not for long. The phone rings again. This time it's Harlan Davis, the shipping department manager. Harlan wants to know if Mr. Moore has approved the vacation schedule of the shipping department personnel. Harlan needs the information because one of the shipping clerks is due to go on vacation tomorrow. Mr. Moore says, "Harlan, do you know how busy I am? I can't be bothered with that now. Put your request in writing. Good-bye."

Harlan is understandably upset. The request he made was not unreasonable, and he needed Mr. Moore's decision. Harlan had sent the vacation schedule to Mr. Moore over a week ago.

Whether he likes it or not, Harlan is part of a communication breakdown. The breakdown developed because Mr. Moore was overloaded with information. What do you think Harlan should do now? Write your answer in the space provided below.

_____

_____

_____

In the final section of this chapter, on pages 51–53, different ways of overcoming the problem of information overload will be discussed.

The Negative Influence of Other People

The third major barrier to effective upward communication is caused by individuals who are susceptible to the negative influence of other people. Such individuals listen to and believe the negative thinking of others. Many times this negative thinking causes upward communication problems.

George Cann, a cabinetmaker, has a negative attitude toward making suggestions to his employer because of an unhappy experience in

the past. When George first started working at the shop, he noticed something that he thought was unusual. No one at the shop used a special tool called an air router. The router is powered by compressed air, just like the tool mechanics use to remove tires at a gas station. It can save many hours of time in building wood cabinets. George figured that air routers could be hooked up to the compressors being used in the paint division of the shop. So, he asked around to find out if the workers in the shop had ever used air routers. Many of the workers admitted having used an air router, but not at this shop. Thus, George decided to suggest that the shop get air routers for the woodworkers.

When George offered this suggestion to the boss, the boss replied, "No way." "Why?" asked George. "Well, for two reasons," said the boss. "First, the compressors in the paint shop are too small to handle air routers. Second, new compressors cost too much."

George knew that the boss was right. He should have known about the small compressors in the paint shop. Thus, George felt a bit stupid about having made his suggestion.

That was 20 years ago. George has never offered another suggestion since then. Sometimes younger employees come to George to sound out a new idea before discussing it with the manager. Usually George answers, "Don't waste your time. These people don't want your ideas. They think they know it all." Unfortunately, some employees listen to and believe George, or other negative thinkers like him. Such employees rarely try to communicate with their supervisors. These individuals think there is no use in trying simply because others say so. To make things worse, they tell others not to try to communicate upward. This is unfortunate because many of these employees have never even tried upward communication for themselves.

OVERCOMING BARRIERS TO EFFECTIVE UPWARD COMMUNICATION

Learning to overcome barriers to effective upward communication requires that you first recognize that the barriers exist. Then you must take action to eliminate the barriers. To eliminate fear of the manager, you must first recognize the fear. To conquer the barrier of information overload, you must first recognize the overload. To avoid being susceptible to the negative thinking of others, you must first recognize negative thinkers. After you recognize each barrier, you will be in a position to take action to overcome the barrier. This section of the chapter will help you recognize these three major barriers to effective upward communication. You will also learn what actions can be taken to overcome each of these barriers.

Overcoming Fear of the Manager

Even the most honest and straight-talking employees distort and conceal feelings from their supervisors at times. It is a fact that most employees tell their supervisor what they think the supervisor wants to hear. To some employees, telling a supervisor what one thinks he or she wants to hear comes naturally. Because employees want their supervisor to like them, it is only natural that they try to win the supervisor's approval. And most employees believe that approval is won by telling the supervisor what he or she "wants to hear."

Recognizing the Barrier of Fear

Employees try to win approval from their supervisors for many reasons. Here are a few of the reasons. Try to add to the list in the spaces provided. If the supervisor likes you, then

1. working is more fun.
2. the supervisor is easier to talk with.
3. chances of getting a raise or promotion are better.

4. _____

5. _____

ILLUS. 2-10

Work is more rewarding and satisfying when employees feel free to communicate with their supervisor

Naturally employees do not want their supervisor to dislike them. Suppose your supervisor did not like you. How would you rewrite the statements given above?

1. _____

2. _____

3. _____

4. _____

5. _____

The statements you have just written will help you understand why some employees fear the manager (or supervisor). Now you can recognize fear of the manager because you know why it occurs.

Taking Action to Eliminate Fear

Overcoming fear of the manager requires two specific actions. Both actions require you to become aware of *false* assumptions. An **assumption** is something we believe to be true but cannot prove with hard facts. For example, some of the more famous false assumptions in history were:

1. The world is flat.
2. Human beings cannot fly.
3. No one will ever run a mile in less than four minutes.
4. Putting a person on the moon is impossible.
5. An electronic computer will never fit into a shirt pocket.

Some assumptions can be proven to be true, but all five assumptions given above have been proven false. Fear of the manager is based on false assumptions. Other assumptions about communicating with employers are listed in Table 2-2.

	Assumption	True or False
TABLE 2-2 **Assumptions about communications with employers**	1. Employees should tell managers what they think the manager wants to hear.	False
	2. Employees will be punished for being too honest.	False
	3. Employees will be labeled as emotional for describing their honest feelings.	False
	4. Employers want to know the employees' feelings about the work, the manager, and the business.	True

The first action you must take to overcome fear of the manager is *to make as few assumptions as possible*. Remember that if you cannot prove something, anything you say about it is an assumption.

When you make an assumption, a second action is required. *You must test the assumption to find out if it is true or false.* Testing an assumption can be difficult because it involves asking a lot of questions. The class activities at the end of this chapter contain exercises which will help you identify assumptions. The exercises will also help you learn to ask questions. By asking questions, you can find out if your assumptions are true or false.

Overcoming the Barrier of Information Overload

Most managers experience information overload at one time or another. Some managers receive so many progress reports, requests for decisions, suggestions for improving the business, and feedback about employee feelings that communication breakdowns occur almost daily. Of course, not all managers are this busy all of the time. The problem is that an employee may need important information just when the manager is overloaded. When this happens, a communication problem occurs.

Recognizing Information Overload

Information overload is not easy to recognize. For example, suppose you are talking with your supervisor about a problem and the supervisor appears to be listening. By appearing to listen, we mean that the supervisor is looking at you and nodding a bit as you talk. Naturally you assume that the supervisor is listening. This is a dangerously false assumption. The supervisor may be thinking about another problem while he or she is talking to you.

ILLUS. 2-11

People are good at pretending to listen

Some people are very good at pretending to listen. Have you acted like you were listening to a teacher today? Weren't you really thinking about lunch or about your plans for this evening?

A supervisor who is overloaded with information can fool some people. But the listening problem of such a supervisor is not intentional. It is not done to avoid others; rather, the listening problem is due to information overload.

The point of this discussion is that recognizing information overload is tricky. Obviously it can be easy to recognize the existence of information overload if a supervisor is writing a report, talking with people, and answering the phone — all at nearly the same time. At other times, however, recognizing information overload is difficult. For example, you may be talking privately with your supervisor but not really communicating if the supervisor is thinking about other problems. Whether recognizing information overload is easy or not, the action necessary to overcome this barrier is the same in both cases.

Taking Action to Conquer Information Overload

Here again, two specific actions are required to conquer the barrier of information overload.

First, *start by telling the supervisor you have a serious problem* when you need an important decision. In other words, let the supervisor know that you need his or her undivided attention! But beware; this action may not get through to an overloaded supervisor. If you suspect that you are not getting through, push harder for the supervisor's attention. Remember that a communication problem is rarely caused by one person alone. And when you have a serious problem, you have an extra responsibility to communicate it to your supervisor.

ILLUS. 2-12

Conquering information overload

The second action requires you *to get the supervisor to tell you exactly what he or she is going to do about the problem.* Don't accept a general answer like the ones listed below:

1. OK, I'll take care of it.
2. Don't worry, I've got everything under control.
3. Let us take care of it for you.

A more exact answer is required. To obtain it, ask polite questions similar to the following:

1. Just a minute, I'm not sure I understand what you're going to do.
2. I need to get this straight in my head. Would you tell me what you plan to do?
3. Oh, before I leave, would you tell me once more what you're thinking about doing?

A general answer from a supervisor usually means that the supervisor did not listen to you. A specific answer is more likely to prevent a breakdown in communication.

Overcoming the Barrier of Negative Thinkers

Negative thinkers or those who are susceptible to the negative influence of others are difficult to recognize. Judging by age will not help. Some of these people may be 16, 26, 36, or even 66 years old. The only one you can recognize with certainty is yourself. Being influenced by the negative thinking of others may cause *you* to be *your* biggest upward communication problem.

ILLUS. 2-13

Negative thinkers are difficult to recognize

Recognizing Negative Thinkers

To help you recognize negative thinkers, you must be familiar with the reasons why people listen to and believe the negative thinking of others. Three reasons are listed below. Try to add two more reasons to the list.

1. To gain approval or friendship.
2. To buy a negative idea is an easy way out. To try out a positive idea usually involves work.
3. A negative idea sounds like the truth.

4. _____

5. _____

Taking Action to Avoid Becoming a Negative Thinker

To avoid becoming a negative thinker, you must look at upward communication from a positive point of view. The following guidelines will help you achieve effective upward communication. They will also enable you to avoid being susceptible to the negative thinking of other people.

1. Most upward communication systems work. When you don't know if a system works, assume that it does. You will almost always be right. It is true that some businesses have poor upward communication. But you must find this out for yourself. Effective upward communication is too important for you to rely on the judgments of others.
2. If a co-worker tells you negative things about upward communication, get a second opinion. Suppose your car needs repair. The first repair shop you visit estimates the cost at $500. Perhaps you didn't think it would cost that much. Since you are not sure, it would be a good idea to get a second estimate. The second estimate might save you some money. Similarly, getting a second opinion about upward communication may save you from a lot of trouble.
3. Be alert for negative generalizations. A blanket statement like "It won't work" is not good enough. Press these people for specific reasons. After you get specific reasons, you can judge the reasons yourself.
4. Remember that managers make mistakes. They are human just like you. If a communication breakdown happens, give the manager a second chance. You deserve a second chance if you make a mistake, and so does a manager.
5. Think positive! Emphasize that the system works *most of the time*. Negative thinkers emphasize that the system fails *part of the time*. When you think positive, upward communication can be very effective.

Overcoming the barriers to effective upward communication is not easy. It requires much effort. All businesses need effective upward communication, and you can help by putting your knowledge of upward communication to work.

10 CLASS ACTIVITIES
Instant Replay

Write a short answer to each of the questions below. As you replay the answers in class, remember that you are getting feedback on your understanding of the chapter.

Questions

1. What is the meaning of upward communication? Give an example of upward communication in (a) your school work and/or (b) your place of work.

_____

_____

_____

_____

2. Do managers need only positive feedback? Explain your answer.

_____

_____

_____

3. What does a progress report tell a manager?

_____

_____

4. How is your report card like a progress report?

_____

_____

5. Why is it important to ask for help when you do not understand job instructions? Does everyone ask for help when it is needed? Why or why not?

_____

_____

_____

_____

_____

6. Is giving a suggestion to your teacher a form of upward communication? Which would be easier to give your teacher: a positive suggestion or a negative suggestion? Why?

_____

_____

_____

7. List two routine requests made at school or at work.

_____

_____

8. What is the main reason why employees do not communicate feelings to the manager?

_____

_____

9. What are three kinds of feelings that are not shared with managers by employees very often?

_____

_____

_____

Beware of Dog!

BEWARE OF DOG is a sign that some people place in their yard or by their door. The purpose of the sign is to give notice to people to watch out for their dog. In some ways the sign is a form of negative feedback. Those who do not read the sign could get some real negative feedback from the dog.

Our world is full of signs which give important information. Many of these signs are stated in the negative. In the space provided, list the negative signs you see every day. Three examples are given to help you get started.

1. Keep off the grass
2. No left turn
3. No smoking

Now, in the space below try writing some of your signs in the positive. For example, "Thank you for not smoking."

Questions

1. Are some of your positive signs silly? Which ones?

   _____

   _____

2. Which signs, positive or negative, are easier to write? Why?

   _____

   _____

Climbing Up or Climbing Down?

Up ☐

Down ☐

Is this person climbing up the rope or climbing down the rope?

Write your answer to the question above by checking one of the boxes in the illustration. Compare your answer with others in the class.

The rope climb shown above illustrates this point: People look at the *same* event, yet see it in completely different ways. Now read the story below. It illustrates how other people's views of a situation can affect the way a person views the same situation.

Selling Shoes Door to Door

This story takes place before the invention of television and in the days when radio was just becoming popular. At this time many businesses employed "door-to-door" salespeople. (These salespeople were similar to today's door-to-door sellers of Avon cosmetics or Fuller Brush products).

Edgar Hicks was a traveling shoe salesperson. He had recently been hired by the area manager whose office was in Tulsa, Oklahoma. Edgar's territory was a large part of the Ozark Mountains. At that time the Ozarks were thought to be populated by poor and uneducated people. As Edgar was leaving the Tulsa office to drive to his new territory, he met Al Myers, the man whose territory Edgar had been given. Al told Edgar that he was going to have some real problems selling shoes to the folks in the Ozarks. "Edgar," Al said, "Those people are just plain suspicious of strangers and salespeople in particular. Good luck!"

Edgar drove to the Ozarks. He was there a month trying to sell shoes. At the end of the month, he returned to the Tulsa office and quit his job. Edgar told the area manager, "You can't sell shoes to those people. They don't like strangers. Half of them don't even wear shoes!"

The area manager then hired Clark Wilson to sell shoes in the same territory. On his way out of town, you guessed it, Clark met Edgar. Edgar told him of his bad experience and why he quit. Clark drove to the Ozarks and started selling shoes. In a month Clark set a company sales record. He sold more shoes than anyone in the Southern area.

When Clark returned to the Tulsa office for new supplies, the area manager wanted to know how he had done it. Clark said, "Well, there is something nice about going into these small towns. All the people are just naturally curious. They come out and talk and want to know about me and Tulsa and the car. But the best thing is that half of the people there don't have any shoes. The sales possibilities are unlimited!"

Questions

1. How is this story like the illustration of the rope climb?

_____

_____

2. Can some people negatively influence others? How?

_____

_____

3. Why wasn't Clark Wilson negatively influenced?

_____

_____

4. Are there any similarities between this story and students choosing classes at school? What are they?

_____

_____

5. How does this story relate to your own work or your own life?

_____

_____

Following Instructions

The purpose of this activity is to see if you can follow instructions. Your teacher will choose a student to give the instructions. This student will then ask you to draw something in the space below. While the student is giving directions, you may NOT ASK QUESTIONS.

Questions

1. Is it possible to draw what the student asked you to draw without asking questions? Why or why not?

   _____

   _____

   _____

2. How is asking questions in this problem like upward communication?

   _____

   _____

3. How is asking questions like feedback?

   _____

   _____

4. Is it possible to determine that you are following the correct directions without feedback?

   _____

   _____

   _____

   _____

5. What happens when you try to follow directions without getting feedback?

   _____

   _____

   _____

   _____

Case Problem: Concealment

Mrs. Casper, the manager of a store, has always thought of Sue as "the clerical type" of employee. Sue knows this, but she really wants to become the manager of her own store some day. Mrs. Casper teases Sue so much about being a correspondence clerk that Sue is embarrassed to tell Mrs. Casper how she truly feels. Sue is miserable because she is concealing what she feels.

In the space below write an ending to this situation. Assume that Sue takes positive action to solve her problem. Be sure to describe in detail what Sue does to make the story ending a happy one.

Labeling with "Is" and "I am"

Labeling other people results from using the word "is." For example, Jerry *is* a clown or Ginnie *is* freaky. Labeling ourselves results from using the words "I am." For example, "I am slow" or "I am dumb in science subjects." To help us avoid labeling, we can become alert to the use of "is" and "I am." Try writing the sentences on page 63 without using "is" or "I am."

Example: That movie *is* funny.
I classify the movie as funny.

1. This day is lousy.

   _____

2. Sam is not doing his work.

   _____

3. Ricky is afraid of the boss.

   _____

4. My teacher is dull.

   _____

5. Annabelle's car is a wreck.

   _____

6. I am confused.

   _____

7. I am angry.

   _____

8. I am a student.

   _____

9. I am a good employee.

   _____

10. I am right.

    _____

When we say "is" or "I am," do we limit our thinking? One writer believes that whenever we say "is," we tell a lie.[1] Do you agree or disagree? Why? Does this also apply to "I am"? Why or why not? How does being alert to "is" and "I am" help us overcome labeling?

---

[1] D. David Bourland, Jr., "Language," *Time*, May 23, 1969, p. 69, as quoted in *Interact* by Ellis Hays, a publication of the International Society for General Semantics.

Case Problem: Information Overload

On Friday afternoon the manager of a theater received a call from an employee. The employee said that she had forgotten to send in the order for candy and popcorn for Friday night's movie. The movie was drawing extra large crowds, so it was important to have a good supply of candy on hand. The manager said he would take care of it.

After hanging up the phone, the manager continued a discussion with a maintenance worker. The worker informed the manager that he could not fix the projector. An expert needed to be called. This upset the manager, and he immediately made an emergency call to get someone to fix the projector. As a result, the manager forgot about the candy order. When the theater opened and the large crowds entered, only a small amount of candy was available. What little popcorn was on hand sold quickly. Many customers were upset, and the theater lost a lot of money.

Directions: In the space below rewrite this story, using dialogue as on page 53. Add new details to your script or introduce some new characters into the story. Above all, be sure to apply sound principles of upward communication. After you have finished, read your script to the entire class.

Apples

This activity shows that recognizing negative thinkers is not easy.[2] It should also help you to avoid being a negative thinker.

Directions

Bring an apple (peanuts in shells may be substituted) to class.
Study your apple carefully. Notice its shape, size, and color. Does it have soft spots or bruises? Are there any flaws on your apple?
Place your apple in a bag or basket with five or ten other apples. Mix up the apples.
After mixing the apples, try to find your apple.

Questions

1. Were you able to find your own apple? Why?

   _____

2. In what ways are people like apples?

   _____

3. If some of the apples represented negative thinkers, could you recognize them by just looking?

   _____

4. Is there a difference between the outside looks of the apple and its inside? How does this difference apply to people?

   _____

   _____

5. Are you like your apple? Are there some parts of your life that could use a little polish?

   _____

   _____

   _____

[2]This activity was often used in the classes of the late Professor Irving Lee of Northwestern University.

Communication from Employers

As you learned in Chapter 2, communication to employers is called upward communication. This chapter focuses on communication *from* employers. It is called downward communication. Read the chapter carefully, then complete the activities at the end of the chapter. By reading this chapter you will find answers to these questions:

- What are the most effective and least effective methods of downward communication?
- What are the five types of downward communication?
- Why do people try to cover up mistakes?
- Do employers withhold information from employees?
- What can employees do to improve downward communication?

DEFINITION OF DOWNWARD COMMUNICATION

Communication from a superior to a subordinate is referred to as **downward communication**. An employee is a subordinate, and a superior is another term for supervisor, manager, or employer. When a supervisor communicates to you, downward communication takes place. In a similar manner, when business owners communicate to a supervisor, downward communication happens. "Downward" is merely a term used to indicate the flow of communications. Illustration 3-1 on page 68 shows an example of downward communication.

ILLUS. 3-1

Downward communication means messages sent from a superior to a subordinate

Methods of Downward Communication

Downward communication is achieved by using one or more of four methods. These methods are: (1) oral, (2) written, (3) combined oral and written, and (4) visual.

Oral Communication

When a manager and an employee are speaking face to face, oral communication is taking place. They could also be speaking to each other over the telephone. Oral communication has the advantages of being fast and being adjustable to a person's mood. Can you think of a reason why face-to-face communication might need to be adjusted?[1] Write your answer in the space below.

_____

_____

Written Communication

A letter or memo from an employer to an employee is not the only example of downward written communication. Company magazines,

---

[1]A person may indicate lack of understanding by confused facial expression. Another reason for adjusting might be that a person becomes angry and it is then a good idea to temporarily change the subject.

messages posted on bulletin boards, newsletters, and weekly bulletins are other forms of downward written communication. The message that the employer wants to send is usually thought through carefully before it is put in writing. An advantage of written communication is that both employer and employee can refer back to it at any time.

Combined Oral and Written Communication

The most common example of combined oral and written communication is a situation where a report is being presented at a meeting. Another example is the situation where a manager reads orders and instructions to employees, gives a written copy of the instructions to them, and discusses the instructions with them.

Visual Communication

The visual method of downward communication is most often used in training programs. For example, a film on safety might be shown to a group of new employees. Other types of visual communication include posters, television, slides, and charts. Visual communication has the advantage of giving a message more vividly or dramatically than written communication.

Effective and Ineffective Forms of Downward Communication

Experts who study the methods of downward communication find the oral method the most common. The *most effective* method is the *combined oral and written* downward communication. The least effective methods are downward written communication in the form of pamphlets and reading matter in racks, and visual communication in the form of morale posters. Table 3-1 contains a list of effective and ineffective forms of downward communication.

TABLE 3-1	Effective Forms	Ineffective Forms
Effective and ineffective forms of downward communication	1. Letters sent to employees' homes 2. Notices on bulletin boards 3. Small group meetings 4. Magazines for supervisors 5. Magazines for employees	1. Morale posters 2. Pamphlets 3. Pay inserts 4. Reading matter in racks 5. News stories in the local paper

TYPES OF DOWNWARD COMMUNICATION

Downward communications from employers to employees are divided into five types: (1) job instructions, (2) job rationale, (3) company procedures and practices, (4) company goals, and (5) employee performance appraisals.

Job Instructions

Job instructions are detailed orders or directions about a person's work. The purpose of these precise, or step-by-step, instructions is to help employees do a good job. Employees get job instructions from one or more of the following sources:

1. Direct or written orders from superiors.
2. Special training sessions.
3. Training manuals or books.

Most employees get job instructions before they start working on a new job or on a new part of a job. Phillis Celler works in the sales division of a company which sells and rents computers (see photo on next page). Whenever the company markets a new computer, Phillis must go to training sessions before she tries to sell it. At these special training sessions Phillis uses a training manual to learn about the new computer. The training manual also contains tips on how salespeople can tell customers about the new computer. In this example Phillis receives job instructions by attending special training sessions and by reading training manuals.

Job Rationale

Rationale is a term which means "reasons why." So, a **job rationale** is a reason why someone does a certain type of work. A job

rationale is also concerned with how one job fits in with other jobs. Some employees know what they are supposed to do, but they do not know how their job relates to other jobs at the business.

Mark and Sally work at a toy factory. Sally is a production employee who sprays paints on toys. Mark is a shipping and receiving

ILLUS. 3-2

WE NEED MORE PAINT!

YOU'LL HAVE TO STOP WORKING.

PAINT

clerk. Almost daily, Mark receives shipments of paint. He makes sure that the paint is delivered to paint rooms inside the factory. Mark did not realize the importance of the paint deliveries until one day when they were not delivered to the paint rooms. Mark had some rush orders to process, so he decided that the paint deliveries could wait a while that morning.

In the paint room Sally and her crew were getting out the spray equipment. When Sally went to get some paint, she discovered that only one large drum (100 liters) was there. That drum did not even contain enough paint to get started. Without sufficient paint, a large portion of the production line had to be stopped. Mark didn't realize that 25 employees would not be working if the paint were not delivered on time.

Procedures and Practices

A third type of downward communication is information about business procedures and practices. Such information relates to policies, rules, and benefits. Company policies often deal with both customers and employees. Company rules and benefits are for employees only.

Two company policies dealing with customers are listed below. Add two more to the list.

1. Guaranteed customer satisfaction.
2. No refunds without a receipt.

3. _____

4. _____

Company rules could include the three items listed below. Try to add two more rules to the list.

1. Hard-hat area — All who enter this area must wear special headgear.
2. No smoking or open flame in this area.
3. Breaks are limited to 10 minutes in the lounge. An additional five minutes is allowed for commuting time.

4. _____

5. _____

Company benefits might include the three items listed below. Try to add two more benefits to the list.

1. Vacation with pay.
2. Profit-sharing plan.
3. Paid health insurance.

4. _____

5. _____

The difference between a company procedure and a company practice can be illustrated with information about vacations. A company procedure informs employees on *how* to request vacation days. Company practice informs them about vacation days granted.

Company Goals

The fourth type of downward communication is concerned with company goals. This type of downward communication involves more than just telling employees what the company goals are. The purpose of communicating company goals is to help employees understand the overall purpose of the business. For example, an oil company's goal may be to drill for oil and at the same time keep the environment clean. Insurance companies point out that they are ready to help people.

Your school district is similar to a business. The board of education (like a business's board of directors) communicates certain goals down to the teachers. Do you know any of the general goals of your school system? Try to write a good general goal for your school in the space below. Compare your answer with that of others. And compare your goal to the actual goals of the school district.

A general goal for my school: _____

_____

Communicating company goals is important. Employees who understand the goals of the company develop a strong commitment to it. And employees who are committed to a company are happier, harder working, and more loyal than uncommitted employees.

Performance Appraisal

Performance appraisal is a business term describing the evaluation of employees at work. As a student you are familiar with teachers' grading your work. In business, managers grade or evaluate employees' work, too.

Performance appraisals have two purposes. One purpose is to evaluate employees when salary raises become due. Another purpose is to help employees become better workers.

The two purposes of performance appraisal are usually achieved at two separate occasions. Suppose that an employee and employer meet to discuss the employee's past job performance. Before or during the meeting, the employer will complete an evaluation form similar to that shown in Illustration 3-3 on page 74. Then, based on this evaluation, the employee might receive a salary increase. Several weeks later, the employee and employer might meet again. This time the meeting might center on a discussion of the employee's strengths and weaknesses. The purpose of this discussion is to help the employee improve future job performance.

Performance appraisal meetings can be difficult. Some managers are not very good at talking with employees about improving job performance. And some employees are not very good at listening to or talking

EMPLOYEE EVALUATION FORM   RATING FOR _____

DEPT. CLOCK NO.	INSTRUCTIONS
	1. Disregard your personal feelings. Judge this employee on the qualities listed below. 4. Using your own careful judgment — check the phrase in each factor that is typical.
	2. Study the definitions of each factor, and the various phases of each before rating. 5. If employee performs no supervision — do not rate additional factor for supervisory ability.
	3. Call to mind instances that are typical of employee's work and actions. 6. Explain on reverse side any unusual characteristic not covered in regular factors.

	FACTOR	RANGE					RATING
1	**QUALITY** Performance in meeting quality standards	Careless /4	Just gets by /8	Does a good job /12	Rejects and errors rare /16	Exceptionally high quality /20	
2	**JOB KNOWLEDGE** Understanding in all phases of work	Expert in own job and several others /25	Expert but limited to own job /20	Knows job fairly well /15	Improvement necessary — just gets by /10	Inadequate knowledge /5	
3	**QUANTITY** Output of satisfactory work	Turns out required amount but seldom more /8	Frequently turns out more than required amount /12	Slow — output is seldom required amount /4	Exceptionally fast; output high /20	Usually does more than expected /16	
4	**DEPENDABILITY** Works conscientiously according to instructions	Dependable; no checking necessary /20	Very little checking /16	Follows instructions /12	Frequent checking /8	Continuous checking and follow-up /4	
5	**INITIATIVE** Thinks constructively and originates action	Good decisions and actions but requires some supervision /9	Minimum of supervision /12	Thinks and acts constructively; no supervision required /15	Requires constant supervision /3	Fair decisions — routine worker /6	
6	**ADAPTABILITY** Ability to learn and meet changed conditions	Prefers old methods; does not remember instructions /3	Learns slowly; reluctant to change /6	Normal ability; routine worker /9	Short period for mental adjustment; willing to change /12	Learns rapidly — adjusts and grasps changes quickly /15	
7	**ATTITUDE** Willingness to cooperate and carry out demands	Good team worker /10	Cooperative /8	Limited cooperation /6	Passive resistance /4	Poor cooperation; argumentative /2	
8	**ATTENDANCE** Amount of excessive absenteeism	2 to 3 days normal or 2 days own accord /6	1 to 2 days normal or 1 day own accord /8	No days lost /10	3 to 4 days normal or 3 days own accord /4	More than 4 days absence /2	
9	**SAFETY AND HOUSEKEEPING** Compliance with safety and housekeeping rules	Safe and orderly worker; equipment well cared for /10	Workplace clean and safe /8	Occasional warning about safety and orderliness /6	Warned repeatedly about safety and cleanliness /4	Area dirty; safety rules ignored /2	
10	**POTENTIALITY** Potential ability to lead and teach others	Has no more growth /2	Future growth doubtful /4	Slow development ahead /6	Bright future growth /8	Exceptional possibilities /10	
11	**PERSONALITY** Ability to get along with associates	Disagreeable /2	Difficult to get along with /4	Average or reasonable /6	Well liked and respected /8	Winning personality /10	
12	**SUPERVISORY ABILITY** Additional rating for supervisors only	Poor organization and planning /7	Inadequate supervision /14	Nothing outstanding /21	Good planning and effective organization /28	Outstanding leadership /35	

Date rated _____   Signed _____   TOTAL _____

USE SPACE ON REVERSE SIDE FOR REMARKS. EXPLAIN ANY RATING THAT IS ABNORMALLY LOW OR EXCEPTIONALLY HIGH

Factory Management and Maintenance

ILLUS. 3-3

Sample employee evaluation form

about improving their work. Because of these and other problems, many managers choose to have one short meeting with an employee. The purpose of the meeting is to discuss three things:

1. Past job performance (at least a month, but not more than a year).
2. The amount of salary increase (for the next three months, six months, or year).
3. Future job performance, with emphasis on specific things to improve.

Because it is sometimes hard to give or listen to criticism, performance appraisal is the most difficult type of downward communication.

RECEIVING NEGATIVE FEEDBACK

In Chapter 2 we discussed how employees *give* negative feedback to employers. We will now discuss how employees *receive* negative feedback from employers. It is not easy to give negative feedback, and it is certainly not much fun to receive it. However, if we are to improve and become better employees, we must learn how to deal with negative feedback from our employer.

Types of Negative Feedback

Employers give employees two types of negative feedback. The difference between the two is not always clear, but the difference is important. The first type of negative feedback relates to **matters of fact**. The second type of negative feedback deals with **matters of judgment**. Feedback relating to facts is much easier to receive and act upon than feedback relating to judgments.

Matters of Fact

The illustration below shows an employee, Barry, who is receiving negative feedback relating to matters of fact.

ILLUS. 3-4

Negative feedback on matters of fact

Employer: Barry, I've been looking over this invoice for the stereo equipment.

Barry: Yes?

Employer: There are a few mistakes here.

Barry: Oh, what are they?

Employer: Well, the total amount should be $1,120—not $1,110. We received three sets of speakers, not two sets. In addition, we received the sets today, right?

Barry: Yes.

Employer: Well, today is January 27, not January 28. You have the date wrong.

Barry: I'll be more careful next time.

In this example Barry made three mistakes. What were they?

Mistake #1: _____

Mistake #2: _____

Mistake #3: _____

All three mistakes are clear to both Barry and the employer. There is no doubt that the date should have been January 27, that three sets of speakers were received, and that the invoice totals $1,120. Mistakes like these are related to matters of fact for two reasons. First, the mistakes are measurable. The invoice totals $1,120, not $1,110. Three sets of speakers are three sets, not two sets or four sets or some other amount. Second, these mistakes deal with facts because no judgment or opinion is involved. It was not the employer's opinion that the shipment was received on January 27. The day is either January 27 or it is not.

Matters of Judgment

Negative feedback is often based on judgments. A judgment is a statement based on personal opinions. Here is an example where Raquel, a store clerk, receives negative feedback involving matters of judgment.

Employer: Raquel, I would like to talk to you about the luggage display you set up this morning.
Raquel: Yes?
Employer: There are a few mistakes here.
Raquel: Oh, what are they?
Employer: Well, the display just doesn't look right. Try it again.
Raquel: OK.

The mistake in this example is much less clear than in the previous example. Raquel did not know that she set up the display incorrectly. When she finished arranging the luggage, the display looked attractive to her. However, it did not please her employer. But was the display wrong? Let's continue this example with more information.

Employer: The display looks much better this time. I see that the manager is back from lunch now. I'll be going out. See you after lunch.
Manager: Hi, Raquel. Say, I'd like to talk with you about this display.
Raquel: Yes?
Manager: Well, you've got it set up wrong! Here, let me show you how it would look better. (The manager rearranges the display.)
Raquel: You're not going to believe this, but. . .

Differences Between Facts and Judgments

The differences between facts and judgments may seem very clear. Matters of fact do not involve judgments. Matters of judgment are strictly opinions. Mistakes which involve matters of fact are easily corrected. The correction is simple because what one has to do is quite clear. In Barry's case he only needed to re-add the invoice, recount the number of speakers, and recheck the calendar for the right date. Raquel did not have it so easy. The right way to set up the display at first seemed clear. At least it was clear to her. Then the employer and the manager each had different opinions.

Communication problems happen when we treat matters of fact and matters of judgment *in the same way*. That is, in both matters we assume that the right way to correct a mistake is perfectly clear. Because we think we know how to do something correctly, we don't ask many questions. The results of acting this way cause serious communication problems.

To illustrate the problem of treating judgments as if they were facts, let's look at how Dottie, a nurse, deals with negative feedback. The head nurse gave Dottie the following feedback:

Dottie, you have been with us for six months. I want you to know we appreciate your efforts to do good work. I have found three things, though, that you need to work on. First, you spend too much time at the desk and not enough time with the patients. Second, you are not as polite to the visitors as you should be. And, third, you need to cooperate more with the other nurses. We are a team and we need teamwork.

The head nurse was making judgments about Dottie's performance. Dottie treated these judgments as facts. She assumed that the correct behavior was *clear*: to spend more time with the patients, to be more polite to visitors, and to cooperate more with the other nurses. It all seemed so very simple.

Three months later Dottie was fired. She was fired for making the three assumptions mentioned above. Dottie made the mistake of confusing facts with judgments. She thought that correcting her mistakes was as simple as adding up numbers or reading a calendar. Yet, three months later the head nurse thought she saw little improvement in Dottie's performance. Dottie was fired because she thought she could correct her mistakes by answering the questions below. In the spaces provided, write what you think Dottie's answers were.

1. How much time with the patients is "more time"? _____

_____

2. How can you be "more polite" if you are already being polite? _____

_____

_____

3. How much "more cooperation" shows "more teamwork"? _____

_____

Dottie, like most people, guessed she was to do *more* of what she was already doing. After all, she spent time with patients, was polite to visitors, and cooperated with the other nurses. Her supervisor didn't want *more* of the same thing. The supervisor wanted Dottie to do some *specific* things she was not doing such as: to spend more time with the patients when they entered and checked out of the hospital; to be more polite to visitors when enforcing visiting rules, not when greeting the visitors; and to cooperate more by showing a cooperative attitude, not necessarily sharing more work with the other nurses.

BARRIERS AND GATEWAYS TO DOWNWARD COMMUNICATION

Experts who study communication tell us there are about as many downward communication problems as there are people. This is generally true because communication problems are people problems. The three most common barriers to downward communication are: (1) too many links in the communication chain, (2) lack of openness of supervisors, and (3) defensive behavior of employees.

Too Many Links in the Communication Chain

When a verbal (oral) message is passed between two people, misunderstanding may happen. If the message is passed between more than two people, the chance of misunderstanding increases. Should a message be passed between more than four or five people, it is almost certain that some misunderstanding will happen. This process of passing a message is humorously illustrated in the dialogue that appears on page 79.

Colonel communicates to Major:

"At 9 o'clock tomorrow there will be an eclipse of the sun, something which does not occur every day. Get the personnel to fall out in the company street in their fatigues so that they will see this rare phenomenon, and I will then explain it to them. Now in the case of rain, we will not be able to see anything, of course, so then take the personnel to the gym."

Major passes message to Captain:

"By order of the Colonel, tomorrow at 9 o'clock there will be an eclipse of the sun. If it rains, you will not be able to see it from the company street, so, then, in fatigues, the eclipse of the sun will take place in the gym, something which does not occur every day."

The Captain then said to the Lieutenant:

"By order of the Colonel in fatigues tomorrow, at 9 o'clock in the morning the inauguration of the eclipse of the sun will take place in the gym. The Colonel will give the order if it should rain, something which does occur every day."

The Lieutenant then told the Sergeant:

"Tomorrow at 9, the Colonel in fatigues will eclipse the sun in the gym, as it occurs every day if it's a nice day. If it rains, then this occurs in the company street."

The Sergeant then instructed the Corporal:

"Tomorrow at 9, the eclipse of the colonel in fatigues will take place because of the sun. If it rains in the gym, something which does not take place every day, you will fall out in the company street."

Finally, one Private said to another Private:

"Tomorrow, if it rains, it looks as if the sun will eclipse the Colonel in the gym. It's a shame that this does not occur every day."

ILLUS. 3-5

Source: Dialogue adapted from Joseph P. Zima, "The Organization: A Communication System." Unpublished manuscript, 1976, pp. 22–23. As reproduced in S. L. Tubbs and S. Moss, *Human Communication: An Interpersonal Perspective* (2d ed.; New York: Random House, Inc., 1977), pp. 353–354.

While some misunderstandings may be funny, most end by costing time and money. In the following example a business loses not only time and money, but also two very good customers. Mr. and Mrs. Rico went shopping early one morning to buy a new refrigerator. Their old refrigerator had broken down for the last time. Below is the order of events as the Ricos purchase the new refrigerator.

10:00 a.m.   Mr. and Mrs. Rico purchase a refrigerator at a large appliance store on the condition that it be delivered the next morning.

10:30 a.m.   The department manager, who made the sale, gives the order form to Dave, the head shipping clerk.

11:00 a.m.   Dave calls the warehouse and informs the warehouse clerk, Evelyn.

11:30 a.m.   Mrs. Rico calls the store. She tells the department manager that she wants the ice maker that goes with the refrigerator.
The department manager tells Dave of the addition to the order.

1:00 p.m.   Dave calls and tells Evelyn.

4:00 p.m.   Evelyn informs Frank, the truck driver, about the next day's deliveries.

10:00 a.m.   The next day, Frank takes an ice maker to the Rico home.

10:30 a.m.   Mrs. Rico calls the department manager and angrily cancels the order.

10:31 a.m.   Evelyn and Frank are in trouble.

Eliminating Some Links

What do you think is the most obvious way to overcome the problem of too many links? Write your answer in the space below.

_____

_____

If you wrote, "Remove *some* or *all* of the links," you are correct. Yet this simple solution is usually not possible. At work many orders for goods, requests for information, or procedures of the company must involve several people. In the example about the refrigerator, four people at the store were in the communication chain. At best, it would have been possible to eliminate only one of them.

As an employee, you can help avoid this problem in two ways. First, whenever possible, communicate both orally and in writing. Oral communication by itself is not reliable. Second, if you must rely on oral communication, get immediate feedback on the message that you receive.

Getting Immediate Feedback

To get immediate feedback, you must "play back" the message to the sender. To illustrate this process, let's focus on the conversation that might have taken place between Dave, the head shipping clerk, and Evelyn, the warehouse clerk.

ILLUS. 3-6

Dave: Hello, warehouse. This is Dave Barnes at the downtown store. To whom am I speaking?

Evelyn: Hello, you will have to speak up. We're busy here, and I can't hear too well with the noise.

Dave: (Dave repeats his introduction.)

Evelyn: This is Evelyn Alstrom, warehouse clerk. What can I do for you, sir?

Dave: Evelyn, would you please add an ice maker to the Rico order for Model No. Z4C17632 scheduled for delivery tomorrow morning.

Evelyn: OK, Mr. Barnes, will do. . .

Dave: Good work, Evelyn. Good-bye.

Evelyn: Wait a second, Mr. Barnes. Let me read that order back to you. You want an ice maker delivered to the Ricos tomorrow morning. The ice maker fits Model No. Z4C17632.

Dave: No, Evelyn; add an ice maker to the Rico order for a refrigerator. Mrs. Rico called us and wants an ice maker to go with her refrigerator.

Evelyn: I see, you want an ice maker to go out with the Rico order for a refrigerator Model No. Z4C17632.

Dave: That's right, Evelyn. Keep up the good work. Bye.

In this example Evelyn made an extra effort to play back the message to Dave, the head shipping clerk. When Evelyn gave and received immediate feedback, she got the order right.

Some other ways to play back the message include statements like these:

> "Let me see if I have it straight. You want me to. . ."
> "You're saying you want me to tell Mrs. Hill to. . ."
> "Let me repeat that to make sure I have it correct."

Playing back a message takes an extra minute. Yet this extra minute might be priceless to you if it could help you avoid a costly communication breakdown.

Lack of Openness on a Supervisor's Part

A supervisor's lack of openness is another common barrier to downward communication. Openness refers to sharing information. If you are an employee, how would you rate your supervisor on openness? Rate your supervisor by placing an X somewhere on the line below.

10	9	8	7	6	5	4	3	2	1

Willingly shares information. Involves employees in decision making. A very open supervisor.

Says very little. Seems to prefer to keep employees in the dark. Little or no employee involvement in decision making. A closed supervisor.

Downward Communication and the Closed Manager

A **closed manager** or supervisor is one who prefers to tell employees about decisions after the decision is final. Employees, however, like to know about decisions in advance. It is natural for employees to want to feel "in on things." That is, it is interesting to know about our employer's plans in advance. And it is especially good to have advance notice of changes which affect us as employees. Special studies show

ILLUS. 3-7

that a majority of managers usually do not communicate this way. Employees are most often told about the changes or decisions and then are expected to adjust to them immediately.

For example, some office managers spend several hours figuring out a schedule of morning breaks for office employees. Then the schedule is presented to the employees. Suddenly the manager is overwhelmed by complaints. Some employees don't like their scheduled times. Others want to go on break with someone from another department, and they want to change times. Many complaints might be avoided if the manager asks the employees for suggestions *before* making the schedule.

Another example of not involving employees until a decision is made relates to plans and procedures. In a furniture assembly shop this problem is likely to occur almost every day. Here workers are to read plans and assemble wood products such as desks and cabinets. The problem is that written plans made in an office don't always work in the shop. Something may be missing or may be out of sequence in the written plan. When this happens, the assembly process must be stopped and the problem solved. If the planners talk with shop workers before making the plans, the problem might be avoided.

Downward Communication and the Open Manager

Most managers know the value of involving employees in decisions. This does not mean that employees make the decisions. Involving employees means asking them for ideas before the manager makes a decision. This type of manager is called an **open manager**. In some unusual situations an open manager will ask the employees to make the decision. The chart in Illustration 3-8 shows a comparison of the

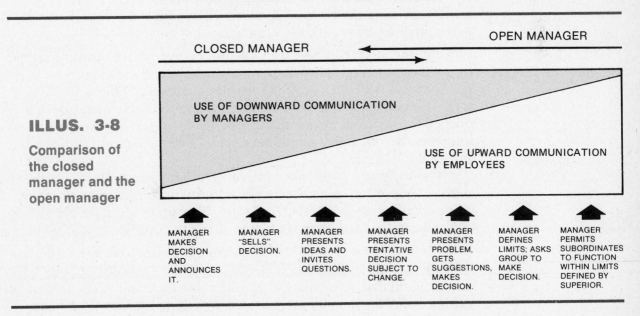

ILLUS. 3-8

Comparison of the closed manager and the open manager

CLOSED MANAGER   OPEN MANAGER

USE OF DOWNWARD COMMUNICATION BY MANAGERS

USE OF UPWARD COMMUNICATION BY EMPLOYEES

MANAGER MAKES DECISION AND ANNOUNCES IT.

MANAGER "SELLS" DECISION.

MANAGER PRESENTS IDEAS AND INVITES QUESTIONS.

MANAGER PRESENTS TENTATIVE DECISION SUBJECT TO CHANGE.

MANAGER PRESENTS PROBLEM, GETS SUGGESTIONS, MAKES DECISION.

MANAGER DEFINES LIMITS; ASKS GROUP TO MAKE DECISION.

MANAGER PERMITS SUBORDINATES TO FUNCTION WITHIN LIMITS DEFINED BY SUPERIOR.

Source: Adapted from Robert Tannenbaum and Warren H. Schmidt, "How to Choose a Leadership Pattern," *Harvard Business Review*, March–April 1958, p. 96, Copyright © 1958 by the President and Fellows of Harvard College; all rights reserved.

open and the closed manager. As you look at the chart, notice how the area of downward communication changes. The greater the area of downward communication, the less the area of upward communication. Because closed managers rely on downward communication, very little information is communicated upward by their subordinates. Open managers, however, receive a lot of upward communication.

At your place of work, you will probably have a supervisor who makes decisions in one of three ways:

1. Makes the decision alone and then announces it.
2. Makes the decision alone and then "sells" it to employees.
3. Gets thoughts and ideas from employees and then returns to the office to make the decision alone.

Remember, a majority of managers use downward communication much more than upward communication.

Defensive Behavior

Many employees find negative feedback hard to receive. We simply have a natural protective reaction to criticism or to being told we are wrong. This protective reaction could be described as a defensive reaction. That is, we get ready to run away from or fight back at the person giving us negative feedback. The purpose of this defensive reaction is to cover up our mistakes or weaknesses. Whether we are reacting to facts or judgments makes no difference when we react defensively.

Kinds of Defensive Behavior

Defensive reaction includes one or more of the following behaviors: (1) shifting the blame, (2) falsely asking for sympathy, (3) denying that a problem exists, and (4) turning against ourselves.

Shifting the Blame. When we shift the blame, we are admitting that something is wrong but that it is not our fault. Remember how Barry got "chewed out" for doing the invoice incorrectly? Barry could have said, "Someone gave me the wrong information." He could have also blamed the addition errors on the calculator by saying, "It's not working properly." Or Barry might have said, "People kept interrupting me, so I couldn't think."

The different ways we can blame others are endless. Certainly some people do give us the wrong information. And sometimes machines don't work correctly. And then, of course, some people simply don't like us. But too often we blame others to cover up for ourselves.

Falsely Asking for Sympathy. Sometimes we admit we are wrong but we try to get the boss to overlook our mistakes. Sympathy seekers hope others, particularly the boss, will feel sorry for them. The process of getting sympathy usually includes falsely asking for help. For example, when Raquel's first luggage display did not please her employer, she could have said, "I'm sorry, but I'm so confused this morning. My best friend and I quarreled last night."

Everyone at some time gets mixed up or just doesn't know what to do. But falsely seeking sympathy and help doesn't solve a problem. Yet we foolishly believe that it allows us to cover up for ourselves.

Denying that a Problem Exists. When we deny that a problem exists, we are trying to act as though nothing is wrong. For example, when the head nurse told Dottie that she was not spending enough time with the patients, Dottie might have replied, "Who says so? That person must be mistaken."

Some employees try to deny that a mistake happened by ignoring it. Ignoring means purposely forgetting to do anything about it. For example, when Raquel was told that the luggage display was not set up properly, she could have purposely forgotten to make a second attempt. Or she might have hoped that her employer would also forget and ask someone else to do it.

Turning Against Ourselves. When we turn against ourselves, we get emotionally "down" on ourselves. This reaction to our mistakes is different from the others. It is different because it does not directly involve other people. We think, "Maybe I am always wrong" or "I guess I'm not smart enough to do this job." When this happens, we begin to destroy our self-confidence. And without confidence, it is nearly impossible to do a good job.

We can choose to use a mistake to destroy our confidence. We can also choose to use the mistake to build confidence in ourselves. Everyone has a choice to go either way.

Reacting Positively to Negative Feedback

When you have a positive reaction to negative feedback, it means that you are trying to improve. Successful efforts to improve depend on two essential actions: (1) you must overcome defensiveness, and (2) you must be able to find out what action to take on matters of judgment. By doing these two things your improvement as an employee is almost guaranteed.

Overcoming Defensiveness. To overcome defensiveness, you must have the ability to recognize it and the willingness to admit only to yourself that you are being defensive. We can recognize defensiveness by remembering the four ways in which people react negatively to negative feedback:

1. Shifting the blame.
2. Falsely asking for sympathy.
3. Denying that a problem exists.
4. Turning against ourselves.

The willingness to admit to yourself that you are being defensive can happen at any time. It happens when we choose to make it happen. Whether or not we choose to admit it, it is certain that everyone gets defensive at one time or another. This happens because some defensiveness is simply a part of being human.

Taking Action on Matters of Judgment. To take action on matters of judgment, you must find out what your employer expects you to do. Remember how the head nurse gave Dottie negative feedback in three matters of judgment? Dottie was fired because she didn't take the time to find out what the head nurse meant exactly by "more time," "more polite," and "more cooperative."

If your employer gave you the following feedback, what would it mean? What would you be expected to do? Write your answers in the space provided.

1. You need to be more responsible.

   Meaning _____

   Action to take _____

2. Try to get things done more quickly.

   Meaning _____

   Action to take _____

3. Do that work after lunch.

   Meaning _____

   Action to take _____

4. Set up a small display near Aisle #4.

   Meaning _____

   Action to take _____

5. Be a little more forceful with the customers.

   Meaning _____

   Action to take _____

Compare your answers with others in the class. Your answers will be different because there are no exact answers. These statements are only examples of matters of judgment. When an employer gives you this kind of feedback, it is difficult to decide what to do. You have at least three choices:

1. Guess what you are to do.
2. Ask a co-worker — in this case you are really asking someone to guess for you.
3. Ask your employer for more information.

Choice three is your best alternative. As you ask for more information, remember that your employer truly wants to help. Employers do not try to confuse employees, nor do they try to make employees guess what to do. Communication errors happen because, like you, employers are human. We all make mistakes. You can help avoid communication errors by learning to be a good communicator.

18 CLASS ACTIVITIES
Instant Replay

Write a short answer to each of the questions below. As you replay the answers in class, remember that you are getting feedback on your understanding of methods and types of downward communication.

Questions

1. List the four methods of downward communication and give an example of each.

   _____

   _____

   _____

   _____

   _____

   _____

   _____

   _____

2. What is the most effective method of downward communication? The least effective method? Which of the methods do you believe is most common? Why?

   _____

   _____

   _____

   _____

   _____

   _____

   _____

3. What are three sources from which employees may receive job instructions?

_____

_____

_____

4. Describe a job with which you are familiar and the associated job rationale.

_____

_____

_____

5. What is the difference between business procedures and business practices? Use an example of each to help answer the question.

_____

_____

_____

6. What is the general purpose of company goals?

_____

_____

_____

7. Do you think employees should know about company goals? Why or why not?

_____

_____

_____

8. Give two purposes of performance appraisals.

_____

_____

Involving the Senses Makes Sense

The purpose of this activity is to show how involving your "senses" improves downward communication. The five senses of humans include seeing, hearing, touching, tasting, and smelling. Of course, one cannot taste or smell most business communications. We can, however, regularly involve our other three senses.

Your teacher will give you additional instructions for this activity. Before you begin, note the labeled spaces in the upside-down triangle below. Write the senses in the spaces where you think they belong.

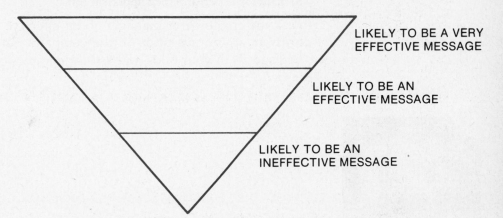

Use the remainder of this page for the group activity provided by your teacher.

It's the Real Thing

This activity is called "It's the Real Thing" because you will bring the "real thing" to class. More specifically, visit with an employer, manager, or personnel manager of a business. Ask that person for a copy or example of the company's:

1. Written job instructions.
2. "Job rationale" program, if any.
3. Procedure, such as employees swapping days off.
4. Goal(s) for this year.
5. Employee performance appraisal form.

Also ask the employer or manager about effective and ineffective forms of downward communication in the company. Show him or her Table 3-1 on page 70 in your book and ask for comments. Report your results to the class.

You're Wrong!

Directions: Read Situation 1 and answer the questions which follow. Then read Situation 2 on page 92 and answer the questions which follow. Look for similarities between the two situations.

Situation 1

Suppose that you and I have a mutual superior who comes to us and says, "This may sound silly, but I'm serious. I want you two to estimate the length of that 2 × 4 piece of wood over there (about 20 feet away). You'll have to estimate because you can't use any kind of measuring device. And you can't get any closer to it than you are now. I want only one estimate between you, but a good one. So, get to it!"

Now suppose the piece of lumber is actually 7 feet long, but neither of us knows this. So, we start sizing up the situation and you say, "Looks about 6½ or 7 feet long." And I say, "No, no — you're way short — that's a lot closer to 14 feet!" Unless you are very controlled, you would probably blurt out, "You're wrong!"[2]

Questions

1. Why would one be tempted to blurt out, "You're wrong!"?

   _____

   _____

   _____

2. Does the story illustrate a disagreement over facts or judgments, or both? Explain.

   _____

   _____

   _____

3. What are the differences between facts and judgments?

   _____

   _____

   _____

4. Which is more upsetting to people: a disagreement over facts or one over judgments? Why?

   _____

   _____

   _____

5. Which disagreement can be ended by finding out who is right: one over facts or one over judgments? Why?

   _____

   _____

   _____

[2]Adapted from William V. Haney, *Communication and Organizational Behavior* (Homewood, Illinois: Richard D. Irwin Co., 1973), p. 65.

Situation 2

Suppose that you and I have a mutual superior who comes to us and says, "After the Christmas season we will cut back on the part-time help. I want you two to prepare a list of the part-time employees. List them in the order of whom we should 'let go' first, second, third, and so on. Now, I want only one list between you — and a good one at that — so, get to it!"

The two of us then start sizing up the situation. You say, "Jim ought to be the first to go." And I say, "No, he should be the last to go." And you say, "You're wrong!" So, we decide to rate the employees on the list of personality traits shown below.

Before going further, study the list of personality traits and check those you think are good or bad traits in a sales clerk. Then compare answers with others in the class.

Trait	Good	Bad
1. Considerate of others	_____	_____
2. Gets things done	_____	_____
3. Quiet	_____	_____
4. Forceful	_____	_____
5. Emphasizes details	_____	_____
6. Stubborn	_____	_____

Questions

1. Which traits caused the most disagreement among your answers?

_____

_____

_____

2. How many in the class rated Trait #4 (forceful) good? _____

bad? _____

3. Are the people who chose the rating opposite of yours wrong? Why?

_____

_____

_____

4. Is disagreement over Trait #4 (or 3 or 5) a matter of fact or a matter of judgment? Why?

_____

_____

_____

5. Assume that your supervisor said, "You are simply not being forceful enough." Would the statement be a fact or a judgment? Why? What action would you take to become more "forceful"?

_____

_____

_____

6. How is Situation #1 like Situation #2? How do the two situations differ?

_____

_____

_____

7. What are the main points (generalizations) to remember about these two situations?

_____

_____

_____

8. Can you relate these main points to a situation in your own life? To a situation at your school or place of work? Describe these situations.

_____

_____

_____

_____

_____

_____

Too Many Links

This activity will show you what happens when there are too many links in the channel of communications. Your teacher will give you additional instructions.

Directions: All participants (5 or 7) will be asked to leave the room before this activity begins. Participant #1 reenters the room first. Your teacher will read aloud the memo shown below to Participant #1. Then Participant #2 enters the room. Without reading, Participant #1 tells Participant #2 about the message contained in the memo. Participant #3 then enters the room. Participant #2 relays the same message to Participant #3, and so on.

In the chart on the next page, write any additions, deletions, or distortions about the message made by each participant as the message is being given to the next one.

Memo

We have a new company policy regarding parking: All employees who drive compact cars or motorcycles will park in the north lot. The west side of the lot is marked "Entrance"; the east side of the lot is marked "Exit." In addition to saving space, the change is being made to prevent accidents like the one involving the truck and sports car in the south lot last week. Company trucks will continue to use the south lot.

PARTICIPANT	ADDITIONS	DELETIONS	DISTORTIONS
1			
2			
3			
4			
5			
6			
7			

Open and Closed Managers

The purpose of this activity is to help you identify the characteristics of open and closed managers. You are to decide if you think the manager in the picture below is "open" or "closed." After you decide, on the blank page at the right write a short story about what you see happening in the picture. Consider why this group of people is meeting, what the manager is saying, and what the employees are thinking. Also write about what you think happened after the meeting. Add as many details as you like. Try to make the story represent a real-life situation that you may have experienced.

Is this manager an open or closed manager?

This space is for the student's short story.

Negative Reactions to Negative Feedback

This activity will help you in understanding defensive behavior.

A student will role-play one of the four kinds of defensive behavior. Your task is to try to identify which defensive behavior is being portrayed by the role player. Use this page as a guide to help you identify the defensive behavior being acted out. Your teacher will give additional instructions.

	Kind of Defensive Behavior	Evidence of the Behavior: Words, Actions, Other Nonverbal Behavior
Role Player #1	_____	_____
Role Player #2	_____	_____
Role Player #3	_____	_____
Role Player #4	_____	_____
Role Player #5	_____	_____

A Swinging Communication Problem

Carefully examine the illustration on page 99. The question you are about to answer requires some thinking. As you answer the question, consider what you have learned about each of the following areas:

1. Methods of downward communication
2. Types of downward communication
3. Barriers to downward communication

Marketing Requested it. . . .

As Sales Ordered it. . . .

As Engineering Designed it. . . .

As We Manufactured it. . . .

As Plant Installed it. . . .

What the Customer Wanted

Question

What steps should have been taken to prevent this communication problem? Consider what happened, what went wrong, and why.

_____

_____

_____

_____

_____

_____

_____

_____

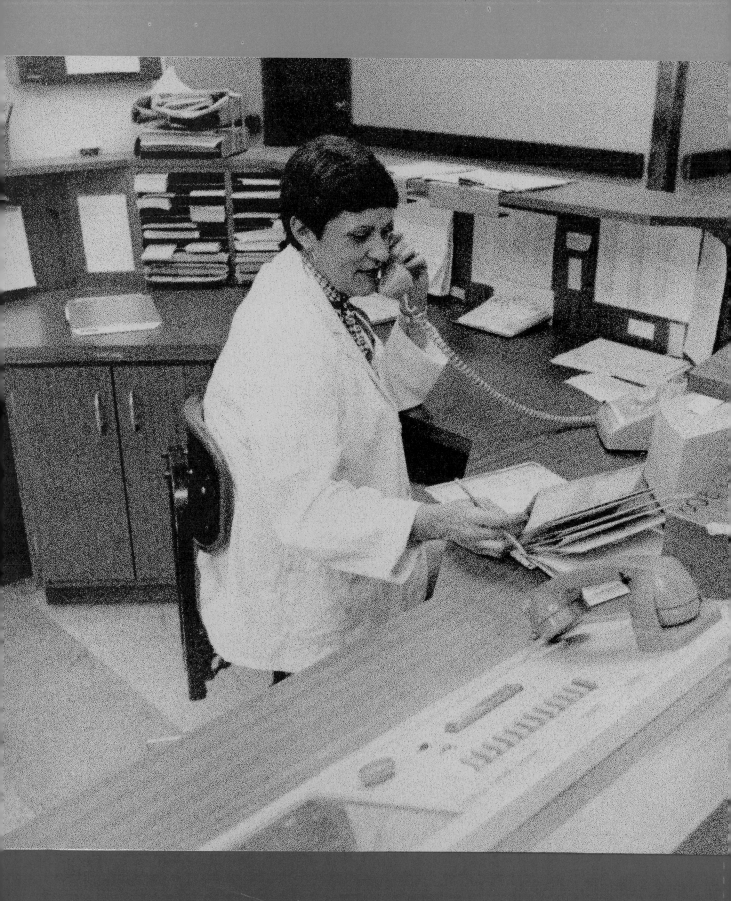

CHAPTER 4

Communicating with Customers

Customers are the most important part of any business. Without them there could be no business. It follows that communicating with customers is also important. This chapter will help you to develop skill in communicating with customers. Read it carefully and do the exercises within the chapter and the activities at the end. When you are finished, you will be able to answer the following questions:

- What are the various types of customer communications?
- Why is it so important to *listen* to customers?
- What are the barriers to effective communications with customers?
- How can these barriers to effective communications with customers be overcome?

WHO IS A CUSTOMER?

Before you can fully understand the importance of communicating with customers, you will need a definition of customers and a description of their roles in business. Very simply, a **customer** is any person or group of persons who buys a product or a service from a business. Describing the roles of customers is best done by using examples. A person buying a week's supply of groceries is a customer. A person buying an airline ticket from Chicago to Toronto is a customer. A farmer buying a new tractor is a customer. And anyone buying a ticket to see a movie is a customer.

ILLUS. 4-1

Various roles of customers

Not quite so obvious, but still customers, are people who purchase health insurance policies and who buy through mail-order catalogs. Even schools that buy paper and supplies for classroom use are customers. In the space below try to write down five different ways in which you or members of your family have recently been a customer.

_____

_____

_____

_____

_____

Now, perhaps your teacher will allow you to compare your list with others in your class.

Why Customers Are Important

The first sentence in this chapter stated, "Customers are the most important part of any business." Why is this statement true? Well, to earn money is the most important goal of any business. This is called "making a profit." In order to make a profit, businesses organize to provide goods or services for customers to buy. When customers buy goods or services, part of the money they pay goes toward profit. It is that part of the money that enables the business owner to stay in business and make a living.

ILLUS. 4-2

Profit is the goal
of all businesses

The obvious conclusion you can draw, therefore, is that businesses without customers could never make a profit. For this reason it is very important for businesspersons to study customers and their needs. Businesspersons must work hard to meet those needs.

How to Determine Customers' Needs

A large portion of the communication between businesspersons and customers centers around needs. As a matter of fact, almost every form of customer communication that you will soon read about has something to do with expressing or determining customer needs. Communicating with customers requires businesspersons to exchange information with customers to determine their exact needs. When this determination is accurate, the result is a satisfied customer.

A very good way — maybe the only way — to determine customers' needs is through communication. Talking to them, reading their letters, watching their nonverbal actions, writing to them, and most important, listening to them will help you to determine customers' needs. For example, a woman might simply come into a store and wait for you to ask her what she needs. A man may drive into a body shop and, after you look at his car, you will know that he needs a fender repaired. A little girl may tell you that she needs a new box of crayons. Or a person may fill out an order blank with a list of items (needs) and send it to a mail-order house. And an insurance agent may write to potential customers asking them questions to determine their needs.

Once you learn these methods of communicating with customers, you will have a better understanding of customer behavior. You will also have a new set of tools with which you can provide better service for customers.

METHODS OF COMMUNICATING WITH CUSTOMERS

Written communication to and from customers, nonverbal communication with customers, and spoken communication with customers are discussed in this section. Listening to customers is such a specialized skill in determining their needs that it will be treated as a separate section in this chapter.

Written Forms of Communication to Customers

As you might imagine, there are several forms in which businesspersons write, or "send," messages to customers. Some of these forms are:

1. Letters or memos.
2. Bills.
3. Advertisements.
4. Signs.
5. Price tags.
6. Product descriptions.
7. Instructions on product use.

Can you suggest other forms of written communication with customers? List your suggestions at the top of page 105.

Because there are so many different forms of written communication with customers, our discussion will center on the two most popular ones: business letters (or memos) and advertisements.

Business Letters

Writing letters and memos to customers takes place every day in hundreds of thousands of businesses. These letters and memos may have many different purposes. The purpose might be to solve a problem, to answer a question, to provide some information, or to say thank you for a favor that was granted. The important thing to remember when writing a business letter or memo to a customer is that businesses are in business to serve customers and to satisfy their needs. All business communication should be done with this in mind.

ILLUS. 4-4

Business letters are among the most common forms of communication with customers

On page 106 is the letter that was written by the secretary in the appliance store illustrated above. After you and your classmates read the letter and write your responses to it, your teacher will lead a class discussion about it.

1230 Morton Street
Lincoln, NE 68504

February 23, 19__

Mrs. Alice Hardesty
5111 Lynn Road
Topeka, KS 68311

Dear Mrs. Hardesty

   This is in response to your request for another set
of directions on the operation of your Zyno TV Video
Recorder. It's too bad that the first set was missing
from the carton.
   I'm sorry to report that we are unable to send you
the material you requested. You see, we only have one
more set of operating directions on hand, and we could
not send it out. I'm sorry we are unable to help.

Sincerely yours

Harold Hanley

Harold Hanley
Secretary

   In the spaces provided, write your answers to the following questions:

1. Did the letter attempt to satisfy the customer's need? How or why not?

_____

_____

_____

2. How could you have improved the letter?

_____

_____

_____

3. What are possible solutions to the customer's problem?

_____

_____

_____

Now your teacher will lead a discussion comparing the different answers given by members of the class. Activity 27 on page 127 will give you an opportunity to write your own letter to a customer.

Advertisements

Another popular form of written communication with customers is the advertisement. Sometimes it is broadcast over radio or television. More often, however, it is written in newspapers, magazines, and other places. Here, as in other forms of customer communication, it is important to remember customers' needs. The main goal of advertising is to sell products or services. But these will be sold only if they are described as potentially satisfying customers' needs. Below are two advertisements (a little silly, perhaps) that illustrate this point.

ILLUS. 4-5

Which advertisement is concerned with satisfying customers' needs? #1 ____ #2 ____

Buy clothing from us so our company will make a big profit and become rich. We need your money so we can stay in business.

#1

Our double-strength flannel shirts will keep you warm and help you look well dressed. Our prices are low and will help you save money.

#2

Hints for Improving Written Communication to Customers

We mentioned earlier that there are many forms of written customer communication besides letters and advertisements. We don't have space here to describe them all. But we can provide you with the following list of suggestions that will serve to improve all forms of written communications to customers:

1. Help the customer satisfy a need.
2. Be concise and accurate.
3. Be friendly in tone.
4. Be neat.
5. Try to write what you would like to receive.

Reading Communications from Customers

A second method of communicating with customers requires some skill in reading. You may have thought that reading skill is developed only for studying and recreation. But reading is also a very important vocational skill because a great deal of written correspondence *from* customers comes to businesses every day.

Examples of Reading Written Communications from Customers

One very common type of message from a customer that must be read is an order for merchandise. There are hundreds of large mail-order companies whose business depends upon employees being able to read and respond correctly to the orders that are received. If you have ever heard a person complain about not receiving what was ordered, you will understand how important it is to accurately read and fill an order for merchandise.

Another situation in business where reading customer communications is very important occurs in a Customer Service Department. Insurance companies, banks, manufacturing plants, and several other types of businesses have customer service departments. These departments exist for the sole purpose of responding to customers' questions, concerns, complaints, and (sometimes) praise. They get dozens or even hundreds of letters daily. And each letter must be read carefully and

ILLUS. 4-6

Customers'
communications
must be read
accurately

handled accordingly. In some cases the customer may need help in solving a problem. In still others the customer may simply need to let off some steam. In any case, it is the job of the businessperson to read the letter carefully, to try to determine the need, and to satisfy it as well as possible.

Hints for Reading Customer Communications

Here is a list of hints that will be helpful to you when reading communications from customers:

1. Read each word carefully.
2. Try to read "between the lines" for any hidden messages.
3. Try to determine the customer's real need.
4. Try to decide what response would be most helpful to both the customer and the business.

When completing Activity 28 on pages 129–130, follow these hints.

Nonverbal Communication from Customers

As you read in Chapter 1, nonverbal communication is the term most often used to describe communication without words. It has been estimated that over one half of all communication is achieved through facial expression, gestures, and body position. There are many ways and many situations in which nonverbal communication can take place. The businessperson may be either the sender or the receiver of nonverbal communication. Here are a few of the different forms of nonverbal communication:

1. Making body movements or motions such as waving, gesturing, and smiling.
2. Maintaining distance such as being near or far from a person.
3. Touching physically such as hitting, hand shaking, and hand holding.
4. Using adornments such as make-up, perfume, hairpieces, jewelry, etc.
5. Employing language "extras" such as laughs, yawns, and special speech qualities.

The possibilities for discussion and activities relating to nonverbal forms of communication are almost unlimited. Our discussion will therefore center on two examples of nonverbal communication from customers: (1) adornments of customers, and (2) body movements.

Adornments of Customers

It is important to be very observant of nonverbal communication from customers in retail stores. Imagine, for example, a woman entering a jewelry store. She is wearing a fur coat and a great deal of expensive jewelry. She has just parked an expensive car at the curb. The jewelry salesperson, Willie, has noticed all of this. Now Willie asks her if she needs help and she replies, "Yes, I need a new watch."

There are several hundred watches in all price ranges and styles in the store. Judging from the customer's statement alone — that she

ILLUS. 4-7

What nonverbal message is this jewelry store customer communicating?

needs a new watch — Willie would have a very difficult time trying to decide what kind of watches to begin to show her. However, Willie has keenly observed this customer so that his job is now somewhat easier. Being careful not to assume too much, Willie can begin to narrow the choice of watches down to a range of the more expensive styles and brands.

Willie has been the receiver of nonverbal communication in the form of dress and adornments. The message that the customer is attempting to send is that she has expensive tastes. She is also saying that she has enough money to support her lifestyle. Willie is probably safe in assuming that she would like to begin her search for a new watch among the higher priced models.

Body Movements

Another example of nonverbal communication is illustrated by a man walking through a department store. He is wearing a loose-fitting coat and carrying a large shopping bag. At first glance, this man seems to be shopping. But frequently he looks up from the merchandise and seems to be wondering if anyone is watching him. Brigit, a salesperson who has been trained to watch for nonverbal behavior, asks the man if he needs anything. He replies, "No, don't bother with me. I'm just waiting for a friend."

As a part of her on-the-job training in her high school distributive education program, Brigit has been trained to watch for shoplifters. Now it seems that the man is behaving like one. Although none of the things about this man automatically makes him a shoplifter, all the

ILLUS. 4-8

The nonverbal message this man is sending is that he seems to be a shoplifter signs indicate the possibility that he is one. Actually these signs, like other behavior and dress, could be thought of as nonverbal communication. This "customer" is unknowingly communicating his possible intention to steal goods from the store.

As the man continues to act suspiciously, Brigit calls her supervisor. Together they watch the "customer." Soon they both see him put a small calculator in his pocket. At that point the supervisor begins to talk with the shoplifter and stalls him while Brigit calls the police. Soon the police arrive and arrest the shoplifter.

ILLUS. 4-9

This shoplifter's nonverbal communication gave him away and got him into trouble

Hints for Nonverbal Communication with Customers

Here is a list of hints for better nonverbal communication with customers.

Receiving

1. Watch facial expressions carefully.
2. Study body movements and try to decide what they mean.
3. Watch for and try to interpret language "extras" such as laughing, coughing, yawning, etc.
4. Notice a person's clothing and jewelry and try to figure out how these adornments affect the person as a customer.
5. Be *very* careful not to generalize and draw *wrong* conclusions based on a customer's nonverbal communication.

With some practice you can become very good at receiving nonverbal messages from customers. Activity 29 on pages 131–132 will provide you with some of that practice.

Speaking to Customers

Anyone who reads about how to get along with customers will soon discover how important it is to be able to communicate verbally

ILLUS. 4-10

It is not unusual to observe ineffective oral communication between businesspersons and their customers

with them. Many of the impressions that customers have of a business have been formed as a result of what they have heard its employees say. Probably more has been written about this method of communicating with customers than any other method. Yet, businesses are still a long way from establishing perfect oral communications with customers!

Using Tact

Speaking to customers is among the most noticeable methods of communication at work. Speaking is also a method of communication that is common and can easily be taken for granted. After all, everyone knows how to talk, right? Wrong! We all make some mistakes with language. Some of these mistakes could be disastrous. Businesspersons can say things that may do irreparable harm to the business's relationship with a customer.

Ellen O'Neil is a stockbroker working for a New York Stock Exchange member firm. She was speaking by telephone to Marla Berman, a new customer. Here is how their conversation went:

Ellen: Hello, Ms. Berman, how are you today?
Marla: I'm just fine, thank you.
Ellen: The Dow-Jones Industrial Average is up 7 points this morning.
Marla: That's nice. Say, I've been wondering what you could tell me about the growth potential of a stock called Ecolotran. I've been watching this stock daily for the past few weeks. It seems to be establishing a growth pattern.
Ellen: That company specializes in antipollution equipment. It does research

ILLUS. 4-11

A stockbroker must be tactful in talking with customers every day

in recycling of waste materials and air purification systems. I feel that Ecolotran is a high flyer, fly-by-night business that has no chance of long-term success. That company is characterized by poor management and no reasonable long-term corporate goals. Mostly because of its potential management problems, I would advise you not to invest in this stock. It will be a loser in the long run.

Marla: Oh, I was just wondering about that company. You see, my sister just joined Ecolotran as a vice-president, and I thought that this stock might be a good investment.

Ellen: Ahhh. . .

As we leave this conversation, it is clear that Ellen has developed a problem in speaking to the customer. What do you think could be the problem?

_____

_____

How could it have been avoided?

_____

_____

If your answer is that the problem was one of tact, or words to that effect, you are right. Ellen did not listen for the customer's need, and she spoke before thinking. Ellen will at least suffer some embarrassment in trying to get back into the good graces of Marla. Or Ellen may lose this customer and her account entirely. The problem could have been avoided by listening carefully and using tact. Tact is a simple word, but it is sometimes very difficult to practice. **Tact** means carefully weighing each word and phrase before you say it to make certain that you give an appropriate response. Had Ellen used tact in her telephone conversation, she would have had a much more successful communication with Marla.

Speaking Precisely

Preciseness means saying exactly what you mean. It is a trait in spoken communication that will give good results. Here is a conversation between Alex, a salesperson in a garden store, and a customer.

Alex: (To the customer, who is considering the purchase of a dwarf apple tree) This is a dwarf Jonathan apple tree. Do you have any dwarf fruit trees?

Ruby: No, I don't have any dwarf trees, and I really don't know much about them. Could you help me by telling me about dwarf trees?

Alex: Certainly. Dwarf trees are like other trees except that they are smaller. They grow to only about 8 to 10 feet high. They have several advantages over larger trees. First, they fit into a smaller space so that you can have a larger variety of fruit trees in the same space. Second, you

ILLUS. 4-12

Precise oral communication with customers leaves little room for misunderstanding later

can pick the fruit of dwarf trees without using a ladder. Third, dwarf trees bear fruit sooner — sometimes after only two years.

Ruby: That sounds very good. Why are they smaller?

Alex: That's because of the grafting process used. Look at the diagram. The nursery people take a regular fruit tree (apple, pear, peach, etc.) and graft a substitute trunk on it from a tree that doesn't grow very large. They then graft a sturdy root to the new trunk to complete the new dwarf tree. The dwarf tree trunk will not allow the top of the tree to grow very large.

Ruby: How should I care for the dwarf tree?

Alex: You should follow the planting instructions exactly. Be sure to get the tree planted at the correct depth. After that, water the tree and apply fruit tree fertilizer every week during spring. After the tree starts to bear fruit, you should spray it once a week from March to August with an all-purpose orchard spray to control insects.

Ruby: Thank you very much for your help. I would like to buy three of these dwarf Jonathans, please.

Alex: OK, I'll put them in a package for you.

This conversation illustrates a precise salesperson. Alex's talk was complete and exact in detail. There should be no misunderstanding on the part of the customer about the dwarf trees or their care.

Rules for Good Spoken Communication

You have just read about two guidelines to better spoken communication with customers. See the list on page 117 for other guidelines.

Communicating at Work

> **1.** Use tact.
> **2.** Be precise.
> **3.** Speak clearly.
> **4.** Work to be understood.
> **5.** Don't mumble.
> **6.** Avoid slang.

Good speech is especially valuable for young employees. Activity 30 on page 133 will give you an opportunity to practice speaking to customers.

LISTENING TO CUSTOMERS

As a communication skill, listening is more important to a person at work than any other communication skill. We have already stated that the main job of businesspersons is to satisfy their customers' needs. And the most prominent method of discovering those needs is by LISTENING to customers. As we stated earlier, we feel that the subject of listening merits a major section in this chapter on communicating with customers.

ILLUS. 4-13

It has been estimated that the average employee spends almost half of communication time listening

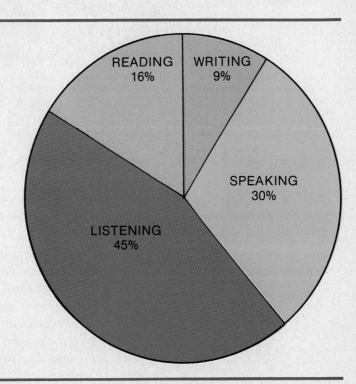

READING 16%

WRITING 9%

SPEAKING 30%

LISTENING 45%

What is listening, anyway? Is it hearing what others are saying? Yes, but it is much more than that. Listening also means **processing**, or working to understand what is being said. Processing is important because people sometimes don't really say what they mean. For example, have you ever heard someone say, "Isn't he charming!" when this person really meant to say, "Wasn't that a rude thing he just did!" Or, "My, how funny!" when the person who said that really meant to say, "That wasn't a very humorous thing to do!" These are simple examples. Sometimes the difference between what people say and what they mean is a lot less obvious and a lot more subtle. It takes active listening to catch these subtleties.

Listening is *work*, and that is the crux of listening skill. Psychological tests have shown that good listening is as much work as speaking, reading, or writing. Thus, at your place of work you must be constantly alert to what customers are saying and to what they *mean*.

ILLUS. 4-14

Most people can hear, but many do not listen

Some people are able to block out sounds and actually not listen to them. Examples of such sounds are those produced by refrigerator motors, lawn mowers, train whistles, jet engines, radio commercials, and raindrops falling on windows. Other people are able, with the same amount of skill, to block out some remarks that others make. Perhaps they hear these remarks, but they don't really listen. When communicating with customers, you must guard against blocking out some words they are saying.

Here is an example of a conversation between Shana, a receptionist at an insurance office, and Akio, a client (customer):

Shana: (Answering the telephone) McKinley, McFarland, and McDougal.
Akio: (Sounding very worried) I would like to speak with Ms. McKinley, please.

Shana: I'm sorry, but Ms. McKinley is doing research in our library and has asked not to be disturbed. Could she call you later?

Akio: (Very distressed) I've been in a car accident that I think may have been my fault. The police will be here soon, and I think I need some advice.

Shana: I'm sure you will have no problem with the police when they come. Why don't you call back in a couple of hours.

Akio: (Softly) OK, good-bye.

ILLUS. 4-15

Akio feels that he needs the immediate advice of a lawyer

As you can see, Shana was not really listening to and processing what Akio was saying. What did Shana do that was not helpful?

_____

_____

_____

What should Shana have done?

_____

_____

_____

If you suggested that Shana was perhaps preoccupied and was not listening to what Akio was saying, you are correct. Apparently Shana did not hear or understand the seriousness of Akio's problem and the fact that he was very upset. Shana should have listened more actively for facts and feelings and determined Akio's needs. These needs were for some assurances and advice from Ms. McKinley or even another agent in the firm. Shana might have taken either of two actions that could have solved Akio's problem. First, Shana could have interrupted Ms. McKinley in the library. Second, Shana could have contacted another agent in the firm for immediate advice.

The point of this illustration is that a person at work should actively listen for and process customer (or client) needs. Once this is accomplished, the employee can work to satisfy those needs.

BARRIERS TO EFFECTIVE COMMUNICATION WITH CUSTOMERS

As you know by now, it is very important to be technically skilled in communicating with customers. You must write concisely and accurately, read carefully, speak precisely, and listen to each word that you hear. These skills must be practiced and learned. Yet, these skills are only the first area of concern for those who are interested in improving communication with customers. There is an even greater problem with certain barriers to effective communication. These barriers involve attitudes and feelings which sidetrack people's minds when they should be concentrating on receiving and sending messages with meaning. These barriers are daydreaming, debating mentally, and private planning.

Daydreaming

Daydreaming occurs when the mind wanders off to some topic that has absolutely nothing to do with the communication at hand. For example, have you ever thought about what you plan to do after school while your teacher was talking? Have you ever thought about your summer vacation while trying to read a book? Of course you have. Everybody does some amount of daydreaming, and it is healthy if it doesn't interfere with communication.

One of the main reasons why daydreaming occurs is a mental process called detouring. A person who **detours** is associating something with a spoken or written message. This association can cause you to start thinking about something other than the message at hand. For example, suppose you are an employee in a department store and a customer asks you about ski socks. This customer also mentions a planned trip to the mountains. As soon as the trip is mentioned, you might be "detoured" into thinking about your own trip to the desert last summer. This might lead you to thinking about how your car broke down on the way — which may in turn lead you to thoughts of having your car's oil changed soon.

See how easy it is to detour into daydreaming! Meanwhile, you didn't hear the customer ask you if you had any brown wool knee socks that would fit into a new pair of ski boots.

ILLUS. 4-16

Many times our minds "detour" when they should be concentrating on receiving a given message

Daydreaming is a barrier to communication because it blocks out a given message. It can often occur at work with customers. This can be a very big problem because daydreaming will not allow the businessperson to determine accurately a customer's needs.

Debating Privately

ILLUS. 4-17

It is a temptation to debate privately about a speaker or writer rather than to concentrate on the message being sent

Another barrier to effective communication is debating. In this case debating doesn't mean *actually* arguing the pros and cons of a situation with a speaker or writer. Rather, it means thinking about the speaker or writer's good or bad points instead of concentrating on that person's message.

You may find yourself debating privately for several reasons. One reason is that you may be bored. Another is that you may be uninterested. Still another reason is that you may do it just for fun. Whatever the reason, debating privately causes you to miss receiving the message being sent. This is because your mind is occupied with the "debate."

For example, suppose you are a hair stylist employed in a hair styling salon. One of your regular customers has a habit of bringing you up to date with a pet cat's playful ways. But you are not interested in cats at all. As a matter of fact, you detest them. One day, while you are getting ready to give this customer a permanent, something unusual happens. The customer is telling you about the cat's most recent antics and incidentally asks you to give a $10 permanent instead of the usual $25 permanent. In the meantime you have been privately debating this customer's preoccupation with the cat and are not listening to the request for the $10 permanent. You actually end up giving the usual $25 permanent. Can you imagine the problem you'll have when this customer refuses to pay $25? You may not only wind up paying for the difference in price — you may also lose this customer and your job!

Private Planning

The last barrier to effective communication with customers that we will discuss is private planning. The problem of **private planning**

ILLUS. 4-18

Many spoken messages are not received because of the receiver's private planning

comes about because of people's need to talk. Most people prefer talking to listening, so they spend a great deal of time planning what they are going to say next while another person is still talking. This lack of concentration on what others are saying results in many spoken messages that are never received.

Some private planning is appropriate, of course. Otherwise there would be long periods of silence after each person finished talking while the other was thinking of how to respond. But too much private planning can be a serious barrier to effective communication with customers.

For example, assume that you are graduating from high school next month. You have had pretty good grades throughout high school, you speak remarkably well, and you can type 40 words per minute. Also, you are one of those people who prefer talking to listening. Therefore, you would like to explore a career in the communicating arts, say, radio broadcasting. Since your parents can't afford to send you to college, you must get a full-time job to pay your tuition for evening classes. Luckily enough for you, two weeks ago you saw a publishing company's advertisement for an editorial clerk. Since publishers are in the communicating arts business, you believe that it might not be a bad idea to acquire experience in a publishing company. You therefore mailed your letter of application right away, and in a few days were notified to come for an interview. The interview yesterday afternoon *began* like this (remember, you were selling yourself, so the interviewer was your customer):

Interviewer: Come in, M_____. Please have a seat.
You: Thank you. It sure feels good to sit after standing for more than an hour in the bus!
Interviewer: Oh, yes, buses don't seem to be. . .
You: (Interrupting) And to think that more heavy snow is forecast for the rest of this week! But I really don't mind all this snow. It gives me a chance to take skiing lessons in nearby Sugar Loaf Mountains every weekend. On week nights I enjoy reading mystery books.
Interviewer: That's interesting. What . . .
You: (Interrupting) But I like to read biographies and novels, too. Have you read the latest No. 1 bestseller by Hanson? I've read every one of this author's books. I think all of them are excellent, don't you?
Interviewer: I'm afraid I . . .
You: (Interrupting) I know that I'll enjoy working for your company. Authors are fascinating people to me. I wonder if your authors come by for a visit often.

Do you think you'll be offered the job? Chances are that you will not. Too much private planning on your part occurred when you kept interrupting the interviewer. And most people resent being interrupted too often.

OVERCOMING BARRIERS TO COMMUNICATION WITH CUSTOMERS

The barriers to effective communication just described are a problem in any setting. They are especially harmful in communicating with customers. Customers who don't feel that they have been heard by people representing a business will think that the business doesn't care about them or their needs. Such customers won't buy goods or services from that business.

There is a way to overcome barriers to effective communication with customers. *Control* is the key word. You must learn to control your mind so that it does not wander away from the words or messages sent by the customer. Exercising control is not always easy. Sometimes it is very hard. Controlling your mind takes a great deal of practice, but you can do it.

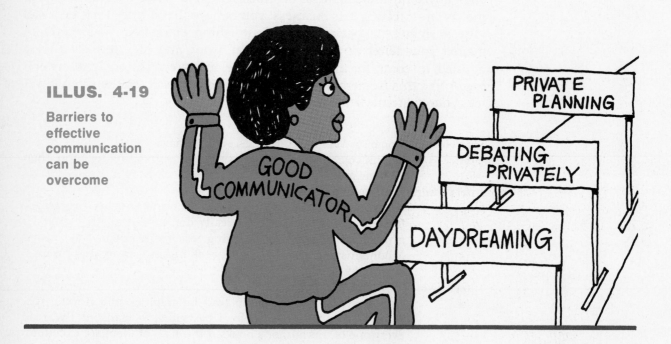

ILLUS. 4-19

Barriers to effective communication can be overcome

Now that you know what the barriers to effective communication with customers are, you are well on your way to improving communication with them. First, you must recognize when one of these barriers stops you from receiving a message. Then you must practice control of your own mind so as not to let it wander. One way you can do this is to pretend that you are going to have to take a test on the message that is sent. This simple exercise should help you to overcome the barriers to communication with customers, as well as with other people. Activity 31 on page 134 will give you some experience in identifying some of your own barriers to communication with others.

26 CLASS ACTIVITIES
Instant Replay

Write a short answer to each of the questions below. As you replay the answers in class, remember that you are getting feedback on your understanding of the chapter.

Questions

1. Who is a customer? Give examples of obvious and not so obvious customers.

   _____

   _____

   _____

2. Why does communication with customers center around customer needs?

   _____

   _____

   _____

3. What are the five methods of customer-businessperson communications? Give an example of each of these types of communications.

   _____

   _____

   _____

   _____

   _____

4. Describe how reading is a form of customer communication.

   _____

   _____

5. What must one do to "read between the lines"?

_____

_____

_____

6. List five examples of nonverbal communication.

_____

_____

_____

7. How can nonverbal messages help one satisfy customer needs?

_____

_____

_____

8. Why might a businessperson get into a meaningless argument with a customer?

_____

_____

_____

9. What is "precise oral communication"?

_____

_____

_____

10. What is meant by the statement, "Listening is work"?

_____

_____

_____

11. Describe how daydreaming can be a barrier to good customer communication.

_____

_____

_____

12. What is a private debate? How does it interfere with customer communication?

_____

_____

_____

13. Describe three ways to overcome the barriers to communication with customers.

_____

_____

_____

Writing to a Customer

Below is a letter from a customer. Read it, and then write a creative letter answering the customer. You may assume anything you wish in your letter, but remember to try your best to satisfy the customer's needs. Write your letter on the back of this page.

```
                              924 Wildwood Dr.
                              Highland, IN  46322
                              April 6, 19__

Ms. Lynn Whiteball
Double-White Bleach
4537 Winton Rd.
Cincinnati, OH  45232

Dear Ms. Whiteball

    I have noticed that after using Double-White Bleach
on my shirts they tend to become yellowish after a few
washings.  Your advertising specifically states that
this will not happen.
    Perhaps I am doing something wrong when washing.
Will you please help by telling me what might be the
problem?

                              Sincerely

                              Jose Cramden

                              Jose Cramden
```

This space is for the student's letter.

Name _____   Date _____

Reading a Message from a Customer

This activity will give you some practice in improving your ability to receive written messages. Carefully read the message below. Then answer the questions that follow and discuss your responses with others in the class.

To the person responsible for customer relations at
Amalgamated Airlines

Dear Person

    A few weeks ago I flew on one of Amalgamated's jets
to North Dakota to visit my grandchildren. Usually I
enjoy flying with your airline. But this trip was the
most miserable one I have ever taken.
    First, your agent in San Francisco was rude to me
and wouldn't allow me to check three pieces of luggage
onto my flight. Next, the flight attendant refused to
find a magazine for me to read. Then we hit some rough
air pockets and I was bounced all over my seat, almost
spilling my coffee. I was also served an inadequate,
cold lunch. Finally, the airplane was 35 minutes late
arriving at the airport. I don't know if I will ever
take an air trip again.
    I thought I should tell you about my experience.

                              Sincerely

                              Harriet Harba

                              Harriet Harba

Questions

1. What do you think was Harriet's real need?

_____

_____

_____

2. What hidden message did you find "between the lines"?

_____

_____

_____

_____

3. If you were the customer service representative for Amalgamated Airlines, how would you respond to this message? Write a brief letter in the space below. Try to make it helpful to both the customer and the airline.

Receiving Nonverbal Messages from Customers

In the space below each drawing on this and the next page, write down what nonverbal messages you think the customers are sending. Then compare your interpretations with those of others in your class.

_____   _____   _____

_____   _____   _____

_____   _____   _____

_____   _____   _____

_____   _____   _____

_____   _____   _____

_____   _____   _____

_____   _____   _____

_____   _____   _____

Speaking to Customers

Your teacher will divide the class into pairs. You will take turns playing a salesperson, telling one another how a specific product will meet a customer's needs. One of the products is an orange; the second product is a felt-tip marker. You should first make a list of benefits of the orange or felt-tip marker in the space below. Then proceed to tell your "customer" how those benefits will meet his or her needs.

Speak precisely and with tact. Speak clearly, and work to be understood. Don't mumble, and avoid slang.

Benefits of the Orange

_____

_____

_____

_____

Benefits of the Felt-Tip Marker

_____

_____

_____

_____

Recognizing Your Own Barriers to Communication

Daydreaming, debating privately, and private planning are all barriers to effective communication. Almost everybody does a little of these things. In order to make you more aware of each barrier, watch your *listening* and *reading* behavior very carefully for the next day. Keep track of your own problems and write down one instance of each form of barrier that got in your way during the day. Once you are aware of these instances, you will be able to control your mind better.

Daydreaming _____

_____

_____

_____

_____

Debating privately _____

_____

_____

_____

_____

Private planning _____

_____

_____

_____

_____

Critical Incidents in Communicating with Customers

A critical incident is a real-life situation which requires on-the-spot action. This activity contains several critical incidents. In each situation a difficult decision is needed quickly.

Your teacher will first call for volunteers. Then the teacher will describe the critical incident. The volunteers must then act quickly to solve the problem.

Use pages 135–137 to record what actions the volunteers take to solve the problem. Also list the advantages and disadvantages of those actions. Finally, describe what you would do in a similar situation.

Critical Incident #1

Action taken _____

_____

_____

Advantages and disadvantages of the action _____

_____

_____

What I would do in a similar situation _____

_____

_____

_____

Critical Incident #2

Action taken _____

_____

_____

Advantages and disadvantages of the action _____

_____

_____

What I would do in a similar situation _____

_____

_____

Critical Incident #3

Action taken _____

_____

_____

Advantages and disadvantages of the action _____

_____

_____

What I would do in a similar situation _____

_____

_____

Critical Incident #4

Action taken _____

_____

_____

Advantages and disadvantages of the action _____

_____

_____

What I would do in a similar situation _____

_____

_____

Critical Incident #5

Action taken ———————————————————————————
————————————————————————————————————
————————————————————————————————————

Advantages and disadvantages of the action ————————————
————————————————————————————————————
————————————————————————————————————

What I would do in a similar situation ——————————————
————————————————————————————————————
————————————————————————————————————

Communicating with Fellow Employees

Effective communication with fellow employees may be the single most important part of "keeping" your job. We say "keeping" your job because most people lose jobs when they fail to get along with fellow employees. Failure to get along with fellow employees is often caused by poor communication.

The purpose of this chapter is to help you to understand both the obvious and the not-so-obvious ways in which fellow employees communicate. Read this chapter carefully; then do the exercises within the chapter and the activities at the end of the chapter. When you are finished, you will be able to answer the following questions:

- What are some management policies regarding fellow employee communication?
- How do work groups communicate general, social, and production standards?
- What is status, and how is it communicated?
- Why do work groups stick together?
- What is the grapevine, and how does it work?

DEFINITION OF HORIZONTAL COMMUNICATION

Horizontal communication is communication between people in a business organization who have about the same amount of authority. This term is best understood by recalling the meanings of upward and downward communication. In Chapter 2 you studied communication *to* employers — upward. In Chapter 3 you studied communication *from* employers — downward. The terms "upward" and "downward" were used to indicate a higher and lower level of authority in an organization. In this chapter you will study communication between fellow employees who are at the same level of authority in the organization — horizontal.

Before reading further, let's be certain that you understand this definition of horizontal communication. Look at the organizational chart on page 32 in Chapter 2 and then answer the question below. Write your answer in the space provided.

Which employees are on the same level in the organization? (Remember that employees on the same level have similar authority and communicate horizontally when exchanging messages.)

_____

_____

As you will learn from this chapter, horizontal communication takes place continually both *within* and *outside* departments or organizational divisions.

Horizontal Communication Within Departments

Within departments fellow employees may talk about employment matters such as the location of certain products and supplies, orders for goods, break and lunch schedules, and helpful information about customers. Sometimes fellow employees talk about personal matters. For example, some of them gossip and others talk about the weather or vacations or their families. Personal communication like this is called **informal communication**, which is discussed later in this chapter.

Horizontal Communication Outside Departments

Horizontal communication between employees on the *same level* but in *different* departments may also be both personal and business in nature. Here is a situation where business communication between fellow employees in different departments might take place. Suppose a customer is unable to obtain a special type of paint at the Home Improvement Department of a large store. The Home Improvement salesperson will urge the customer to try the store's Catalog Department. If the customer agrees, it is important that the salesperson communicate immediately with a fellow employee in the Catalog Department about this customer's needs. The Home Improvement salesperson can do this either by phone or by going directly to the Catalog Department.

As far as business matters are concerned, the most important part of communication with personnel in a different department is to try to keep it horizontal. For example, the manager of Department A may communicate *directly* with the manager of Department B. An employee in Department A may communicate *directly* with a fellow employee in

Horizontal communication within a department
(at the Home Improvement Center)

Horizontal communication outside departments
(between salespersons of Home Improvement
Center and of Catalog Department)

Department B. But an employee in Department A usually does *not* communicate directly with the manager of Department B. The opposite is also true. The manager of Department A usually does *not* communicate directly with an employee in Department B.

Here is an example of the proper flow of communication outside departments. Joyce is a clerk in the claims department of an insurance company. She wanted to attend a company-sponsored program on career opportunities which was scheduled during working hours on Monday. Joyce asked and received permission from her supervisor to attend the program. Then Joyce told Kirk, a clerk in the mail room, about the program. And Kirk decided that he, too, would like to attend it. It would be *improper* for Joyce to ask permission from Kirk's supervisor for Kirk to attend the program. Kirk himself must ask permission from his supervisor. The proper flow, or channel, of communication in this example is shown in the illustration below.

Horizontal communication outside a department is simple and easy if employees follow proper procedures. Communication within the

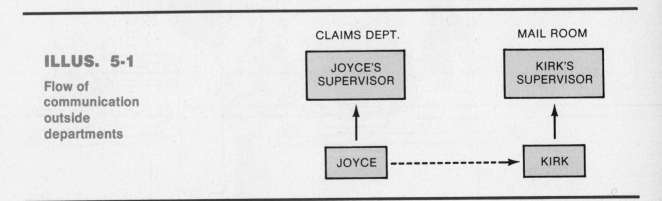

ILLUS. 5-1

Flow of
communication
outside
departments

CLAIMS DEPT.

JOYCE'S SUPERVISOR

MAIL ROOM

KIRK'S SUPERVISOR

JOYCE - - - - - - - - -> KIRK

department is even easier if employees follow the company rules. A company rule which most new employees or newcomers to the business world don't know about concerns management's attitude toward horizontal communication.

Management's Attitude Toward Horizontal Communication

Surprisingly, most organizations — be they factories, offices, restaurants, or hospitals — *discourage* communication of a personal nature among fellow employees during working hours. The reason is simple: If you are talking to a fellow employee, you are not working. This may seem overstated, yet it is generally true. Certainly managers want employees to share information and help one another. But the attitude toward horizontal communication among fellow employees in most businesses is "do it quickly and keep it to a minimum."

Managers in many business establishments actually forbid any type of horizontal communication among employees except during break periods. In these instances management insists that employees ask their supervisor all questions about the work. These managers are not trying to be unkind. They have decided that the supervisor, rather than another employee, has the best answer to questions about work. If you have doubts about these no-talking policies, simply take note of employee behavior when a supervisor is away from a department and when a supervisor is in a department. Most employees talk quite a bit in the absence of the supervisor. But when the supervisor returns to the department, they stop talking and look busy!

ILLUS. 5-2

COMMUNICATION AND WORK GROUP BEHAVIOR

Effective communication in a work group depends on your knowledge of work group behavior. Knowing how work groups behave is especially important to a new employee or an experienced employee in a new job. It is highly desirable to be accepted and liked by group members and to know which of them are "informal" group leaders. A careful study of this section of the chapter will help you understand some less-than-obvious behavior patterns of work groups.

Joining a Work Group

A new employee or an experienced employee in a new job comes to work with several concerns. First, most new employees want to be accepted by their fellow employees. We want others to take an interest in us, and we want to take an interest in them. Another concern of the new employee relates to what the group members consider to be acceptable standards of behavior. We want to know things like: How do group members observe company rules? Do members of the group socialize together? Just how much work will I be expected to do? Finally, when a new employee enters a closely knit work group, there may be a "testing period" during which the new employee must prove himself or herself. This testing period may last a week or several weeks. In all aspects of joining a work group, effective communication is an employee's greatest asset.

Initial Group Acceptance

It is generally agreed that people need people. From this simple truth it is fair to conclude that people desire to belong to groups of people. One of the most important groups in life is the work group. It is important because we spend about half of our nonsleeping hours with members of the work group.

When you begin working with a group, three things should happen. First, the group members talk with you and you talk with them. Second, you are able to take an honest interest in them. Lastly, they are able to take an honest interest in you. If these three things happen, you are initially accepted by the group, or you are "in." If they don't happen, you remain "out." Let's examine some examples of group behavior that result in initial acceptance or nonacceptance by the group.

Fay recently got a job as a ticket seller in the box office of a movie theater. The theater employed two ushers, two ticket takers, and three candy sellers. Fay worked alone in the ticket booth, but she went on break with some of the other employees. During these times Fay talked about the weather or the amount of ticket sales. When the conversation turned to personal matters, such as dating, Fay had practically nothing to say even though she was interested. When asked a question, Fay usually answered, "Yes," or "No," or "I don't know." As a result, her fellow employees thought that she was not interested in them. Three

weeks later Fay quit her job because it was "too lonely" in the ticket booth.

Clara got her job at the Vacation Inn motel about the same time Fay started at the theater. Clara's job was to bus dishes in the dining area of the inn. Unlike Fay, Clara knew the importance of communicating to gain group acceptance. Clara worked hard, but she talked with the other employees when the time seemed right. She asked questions about their hobbies and favorite TV shows. Pretty soon they were asking Clara about the same things. Clara was quickly accepted by the work group because she had taken an honest interest in them and they took an honest interest in her.

In the two examples given above, communication was the key to group acceptance. To show that you have an interest in others, you must communicate. Perhaps it is sometimes unfair, but people assume that those who do not talk with them, or ask questions about them and the things they like to do, are not interested in them. The responsibility to begin communicating with others often falls on the new employee. To be accepted in a work group, new employees must take the initiative by talking with and showing interest in their fellow employees. When new employees do this, the members of the work group will also talk with and show an interest in them. New employees who choose to wait for others to show an interest in them often wait a long, long time.

ILLUS. 5-3

Group Standards

After initial acceptance is communicated by both the new employee and the work group, the new employee may then become concerned about the "rules of the game." The main question is: What does the group expect me to do and not to do?" The process of finding out the answer to this question is called *determining group standards*. A **standard** is simply another word for appropriate behavior.

Work groups communicate their standards *indirectly*. That is, they do not bluntly state or write the rules of the game. Rather, the new employee must find out what these standards are by watching, listening, and asking questions. Work groups do this because not all standards apply to everyone. In addition, the exact meanings of specific standards may not be clear to everyone in the group. Group standards may be divided into three specific areas: general standards, social standards, and production standards. A new employee first learns about the general standards; learning about the other standards follows.

General Standards. General standards describe how the work group interprets and observes company rules. For example, even though the company rule is to allow 15 minutes for a break period, a new employee might observe that members of a work group seem to take anywhere from 20 to 30 minutes. Or the new employee might observe that everyone stops talking when the manager is around. Or, if employees are expected to work until 10 minutes before quitting time and then clean up the work area, the new employee might notice that the group members stop working about 30 minutes before quitting time and clean up very slowly.

Most new employees are eager to do a good job and, at the same time, want to play by the rules of their work group. The question that new employees face is: Which of the company rules are strictly enforced and which are not? It doesn't seem fair to follow company rules which everyone else ignores. But in trying to learn the work group's rules, new employees often take risks. When taking a risk results in a mistake, new employees must be responsible for their own behavior.

For example, take the case of Sam, an apprentice machinist in a shop where work begins at 8:00 a.m. On Monday Sam arrived at work about 7:45 a.m. Most of the other employees were already there, drinking coffee and talking in the employee lounge. Sam joined them for a few minutes. At about 7:55 a.m. he quickly walked to the time clock, punched in, and hurried to his work station. Sam had been told by the supervisor very clearly and forcefully that he had to be at his work station by 8:00 a.m. sharp! Yet Sam noticed that his fellow employees did not leave the lounge area until 7:58 a.m. As a result, some of them were not at their work stations until about 8:03 a.m. All day long his fellow employees teased him about being a "real go-getter!"

On Tuesday Sam decided to punch in on the time clock at about the same time as his fellow employees did. At about 7:58 a.m. his fellow employees began to leave the lounge area. Not wanting to be the first to punch the clock, Sam stood at the end of the line. By the time he got to his work station, it was 8:05 a.m. Because Sam was a new

ILLUS. 5-4 Sam took a risk and got into trouble

Communicating at Work

employee, the supervisor wanted to make sure that Sam developed "proper" work habits. So, the supervisor walked over to Sam and said, "Work begins at 8 a.m. sharp. Don't be late again!"

As you can see, Sam took a risk and got himself into trouble. Some new employees in Sam's situation, however, make an additional serious mistake. When the supervisor corrects them, they usually reply with this excuse: "Well, everyone else does it. Why pick on me?" This excuse causes hard feelings, not only between the supervisor and the new employee, but also between the new employee and the work group. In the first place, the supervisor already knows that everyone else does it. Calling attention to this fact may communicate a lack of respect for the supervisor. The typical response by the supervisor to this excuse is, "I don't care what everyone else does. You do what I tell you to do." In the second place, when a new employee uses the behavior of the work group as an excuse, the group may turn against the new employee. A group turns against an individual when the group feels that it is being attacked. A new employee communicating to a supervisor about a group breaking company rules can be viewed as an attack on the group.

Learning what is expected by work groups and by supervisors need not be difficult. Both fellow employees and supervisors want new employees to be successful in learning the rules. New employees who are willing to take responsibility for their own behavior are quickly accepted by the work group and respected by the supervisor.

Social Standards. A social standard is an unwritten and usually unspoken rule about how to be friendly or neighborly. To "belong" to a work group may require new employees to observe certain social standards. For example, a researcher in social studies observed some butchers

ILLUS. 5-5

who worked in a large grocery store. During their lunch hour, all the butchers except a new one played cards together. The new butcher who neither played cards nor watched the game was considered an outcast. The other butchers rarely spoke to him and generally ignored him even during working hours.

Another study showed that realtors at a small real estate firm maintained a similar social standard. Two or three days a week they all went out to lunch together. Although they generally talked about nonbusiness matters at lunch, occasionally they exchanged some important information about new properties for sale or new and successful sales techniques. A new realtor at the firm who missed the lunches lost friendships and was deprived of valuable business information.

Other examples of social standards at different places of work include membership in bowling, tennis, or golf teams and attendance at TGIF (Thank Goodness It's Friday) parties. Depending upon the activity of the work group, some participation on your part means you are "in" the group. If you don't participate at all, you are probably "out" of the group.

Production Standards. A work group's production standard is an *unofficial* policy about the amount and quality of work an employee does. Work groups are very sensitive about production standards. Employees who are underproducers or overproducers are usually informed immediately of the group's displeasure. Similarly, employees whose work is of poor quality or of too high quality are also informed that they are violating the group's production standards. Of course, *it is good business to set high standards for yourself. It is also good business to desire to be the best worker in the company because your own future with the company depends on your ability to produce.* The point here is that it is simply not good business to try to be "better" than others in the group on your first few days at work.

For example, Roberta was hired as a window washer in a large office building. She was one of a crew of six employees. On her first morning at work Roberta washed 15 windows. At lunch her fellow employees asked her how the new job was going. When she told them that she had washed 15 windows that morning, they expressed surprise. It seemed that most of them cleaned only about 10 or 12 windows a day! They sarcastically asked her if she was trying to work herself to death! Roberta obviously broke the group's production standard that morning but quickly found out the correct standard at noon.

Employees who continually and knowingly break a work group's production standards are subject to extreme punishment. For example, in one company an employee whose output was too far below the work group's production standard had an unpleasant surprise upon returning from a week's vacation. That employee's desk had been rearranged, and a number of needed books and references had disappeared!

Most employees learn the work group's production standards quickly because others in the group, as well as the supervisor, want to help. Work groups are as concerned about new employees as the new

employees are concerned about the group. When you communicate your respect for the work group's production standards, the process of group acceptance will be smoother for you.

The Inclusion Test

The final step in joining a work group might appropriately be called the group's inclusion test. Some groups who are especially close or who have been together a long time do not include a new employee immediately. The new employee must prove that she or he is willing to live up to the group's standards. Thus, the group begins a testing period. As mentioned earlier, this period may last from a week to several weeks. The time factor is often dependent on how quickly the group feels safe around the new employee.

Table 5-1 on the next page contains an overview of the inclusion testing process. Generally work groups "test" four areas of behavior: friendliness to each group member, compatibility with some group members, participation in social activities, and commitment to group teamwork.

If the new employees pass the inclusion test, they are "in." If they do not live up to the group standards or if their personalities clash with too many others in the group, they are "out."

The best way to pass the inclusion test is to know about it in advance and to be yourself. Being yourself is most important. Honest and sincere communication will practically guarantee a new employee's

Behavior Tested	Communications that Reflect Behavior Tested	Group's Hidden Purpose
Friendliness	Commonplace greetings such as hi, how are you? How are things going? (True affection is not involved here.)	To find out if the new employee is willing to speak to us. (Note that quantity, not quality, is important.)
Compatibility	Discussions of personal interests. (Is the new employee interested in things we like? Are we interested in the things the employee likes?)	To find out if the new employee is being sincere or just faking interest in us for the purpose of being included in the group.
Participation	Questions about being included in lunch and after-work social activities. (Does the new employee accept invitations to these social activities?)	To find out if the new employee is willing to give part of himself or herself to the group.
Commitment	Expressed willingness to play the game by the group's rules. (Does the new employee seek help from group members, share the work load equally, try not to be "better" than everyone else in the group, and respect the group's procedures for contacting the supervisor?)	To find out if the new employee is a team player or a loner whose self-interest is more important than the group interest.

TABLE 5-1

Overview of the inclusion test

successful inclusion in a work group. It is almost certain that a new employee will not last long in a group by being insincere.

Status in Work Groups

Status is a term used to describe a social rank or position. In a business organization this social rank or position in work groups is *unofficial*. This means that the formal organization, as shown in the company's organization chart, does not recognize the status systems of work groups. However, almost without exception, fellow employees honor a work group's status system because it serves to give some recognition to each member of the group. The recognition is usually for leadership qualities, special skills, or seniority. Most important, status systems can help or hurt the effectiveness of communication among fellow employees.

Status of Informal Group Leaders

Unofficial leaders of a work group are called **informal leaders**. They are informal leaders because they are selected by the work group, not by the company's management. The process of selecting informal leaders develops slowly and naturally over a period of time during which group members look to certain fellow employees for direction. When a work group is small, it may have only one informal leader. Larger work groups usually have two or more informal leaders.

A communication expert who studied a group of 15 dayshift telephone operators found that three types of informal leaders exist: the social leader, the wage-and-benefits leader, and the technical problem-solving leader. These three are the most common types of informal leaders found in most large organizations.

The *social leader* is a person who organizes the work group's activities for after-working hours. For example, if one of the telephone operators wants to get the group together, the easiest way to do it is to suggest the activity to the social leader.

The *wage-and-benefits leader* is a person who is concerned about the fair treatment of employees in the company. When the operators have a complaint about working conditions, for example, they discuss it with this particular leader. If the company is unionized, this leader is usually appointed by the group to be their union representative. Thus, when the union holds meetings, the wage-and-benefits leader attends and then reports back to the other operators.

The *technical problem-solving leader* is a very skilled employee. Among the 15 telephone operators, this person is the only one who can handle many types of calls, such as long-distance conference calls,

American Telephone & Telegraph Co.

requests for new listings, tracing of phone calls, and special emergency calls, with great ease. The other operators respect this special skill. When they need an answer to technical problems, they usually come to this informal leader.

Informal leaders of work groups are not self-appointed leaders. They neither ask to be chosen nor do they push others aside or "step on others' toes" to obtain the position they hold. Neither are they the toughest or meanest members of the work group. Informal leaders show kindness and respect for each individual member of the work group. A work group allows informal leaders to lead because of respect for their special abilities. Thus, informal leaders have the highest status among group members.

Status of Individual Work Group Members

The status of individual work group members is generally measured by pay, job titles, and privileges. It is management that grants such pay raises and promotions. In some organizations special privileges are also given to certain types of employees by management. For example, production employees in factories punch a time clock while office employees sign a time sheet at the end of each week. Also, some businesses have a cafeteria for hourly-paid employees and a special dining room for members of management. Thus, pay, job titles, and special privileges are the most obvious symbols that communicate an individual group member's status to fellow employees.

There are, however, not-so-obvious status symbols that are communicated by individual work group members to fellow employees. These so-called status symbols usually result from one's seniority on the job. Here are several examples. In some restaurants a new waiter must serve the tables which are farthest from the kitchen. This means that the new waiter must carry the food a longer distance. The new waiter, therefore, has a lower status than those who serve the tables closer to the kitchen. In a machine shop a group of skilled machine operators wear white aprons. A new employee who wears a white apron in the shop on the first day of work is quickly informed by the group that this appearance is inappropriate. In an Eastern city a street-patching crew has an interesting status system: the group member with the highest status rides beside the truck driver, and other employees ride in the rear of the truck. The newest member of the group practically sits on the tailgate while more senior crew members sit near the front, with their backs resting on the cab of the truck.

Effects of Status on Communication

The status of individual work group members or informal leaders has some strong and direct effects on communication. These effects can be both good and bad.

Status Clarifies Some Questions. When a verbal message is passed along from one employee to another, a frequently asked question is,

"Who said that?" This simple question really means, "What is the status of the sender of the message?" For example, suppose the following dialogue takes place between two members of the street-patching crew mentioned on page 153 and illustrated above:

First member: I hear that our work schedule is heavy today.
Second member: Who says so?
First member: Charlie (the new guy riding the tailgate.)
Second member: What does he know!

The response, "What does he know!" shows that Charlie has a low status in the work group. This means that the second member of the crew probably does not believe that the work schedule for the day is heavy. But suppose the first member of the crew answered that Helga, the crew member with the highest status in the group, was the sender of the message. Most likely the second member's response will be: "She is probably right. Better get ready for a long day."

Status Facilitates Communication. The status given to informal leaders often makes communication faster and easier. For example, if a manager wants to send a message to the work group, the manager may tell the informal leaders and count on them to spread the word. Communicating in this manner is especially effective when the manager's message carries negative news, such as dissatisfaction with the below-average output of a group. By simply telling the informal leaders about this bad news, the manager avoids having to call a group meeting where everyone may be criticized. Of course, if the work group's efficiency does not improve after the manager has talked to the informal leaders, a meeting with the group would be in order.

Status Constitutes a Barrier to Effective Communication. Status can be a major barrier to effective communication when people try to impress others with their status. To make this point clear, let's examine three situations which illustrate typical ways in which people try to show off their status. A question is presented at the end of each situation. Write a short answer to the question in the spaces provided.

Situation #1: Condescending Cal

Cal Collins, 22 years old, is a salesperson in a furniture store. He needed some information from the store warehouse and called Joe Allen, the senior warehouse clerk. The telephone conversation went like this:

Joe: Hello, this is the warehouse, Joe Allen speaking.
Cal: Joe, this is Mr. Collins at the store. Listen, this is important. Could you tell me if we have any more of those maple desks, Model #24731, in stock?

How did Cal talk down to Joe? _____

_____

Situation #2: Experienced Ellen

Ellen Franklin is a medical technologist. During a recent in-service education meeting of medical technologists at the hospital, Ellen's comments at the group meeting had little to do with the subject of the meeting. Here is how she answered some questions:

Irene: Ellen, what do you think about our group's problem?
Ellen: Well, I've seen similar problems. Last week I was at a state meeting of Republican women. . .
Alice: Ellen, what is your opinion about joining the morning shift's program?
Ellen: We had the same situation when I was chairperson of our Community Chest program. . .
Danny: Do you have any other thoughts, Ellen?
Ellen: Yes. Jim, I mean Mr. Lewis, our hospital director, was telling me yesterday after the City Council meeting where I presented suggestions for the neighborhood park program, that. . .

What was Ellen trying to communicate? _____

_____

_____

Situation #3: One-up Wally

    Wally Beck is an accounting clerk who shares a small office with three other accounting clerks. The other clerks have 4″ × 5″ pictures of their families on their desks; Wally has an 8″ × 10″ picture of his family. The other clerks have one side chair at their desks; somehow Wally managed to get two side chairs for his desk even though they don't match. The others drink coffee in paper cups; Wally also buys coffee from the machine but puts it in a mug when he drinks coffee at his desk. When one of the clerks brought a small plant to place on her desk, the next day Wally brought a larger plant to place on the floor by his desk.

Why is Wally called "one-up Wally"? _____

_____

_____

ILLUS. 5-8

Trying to impress others may "turn them off"

Cal, Ellen, and Wally each have a communication problem because of a desire to show off status. In their communications, each of them was actually sending two messages: one was the *expected message* and the other was the *status message*. The expected messages were: Cal requesting information, Ellen offering ideas, and Wally sharing his thoughts. The status messages, which were much less direct but just as loud as the expected messages, were really saying, "I am important" or "I have status." The effect of these status messages may confuse communications. In fact, they may even block the expected messages. As a result, Cal may not get the important information he needs; Ellen's ideas may not be accepted by the others; and Wally's fellow employees may not want him to share any of his thoughts with them.

Why Work Groups Stick Together

Work groups stick together because of close personal friendships and loyalty to the group. Personal friendships are usually developed among the people who communicate with one another most often. For example, we may find at least one person in a work group with whom it is very easy to communicate. The more we communicate with this person, the more we tell about ourselves. We speak our true feelings because we trust this person. As a result of the personal friendship, we develop an attitude of cooperation. That is, we want to help and we can expect help from this person.

Loyalty to a work group is much like a close personal friendship in two ways. First, we are loyal to a work group because we don't want to "let our friends down." This expression describes teamwork and loyalty in its highest form. Second, by being loyal we give to and receive from the group a form of protection. If problems develop, we will protect the group and we know that the group will protect us.

Thus, when work groups stick together, they communicate two kinds of attitudes: a cooperative attitude and a protective attitude. Let's examine some ways of communicating cooperation and protection in work groups.

Communicating a Cooperative Attitude

In many situations the best way to communicate a cooperative attitude is to tell a fellow employee that you want to help and then to start helping. For example, take the case of Bruce, a hair stylist. When Bruce doesn't have a customer, he sweeps up hair from the floor. Bruce sweeps up not only his area, but the entire shop. Sometimes, Bruce goes to the waiting area and talks with his fellow stylists' customers. He even offers to get them some coffee or tea from the machines. Bruce is not required to sweep the entire shop or to make his fellow stylists' customers comfortable. He could stay in his own area and wait for his next customer. But Bruce knows what teamwork means. He wants the shop and his fellow employees to be successful. He shows this by communicating with both words and actions.

Here is Bruce communicating a cooperative attitude.

Communicating a Protective Attitude

A work group can be very protective of its individual members. Greg was the least competent member among 23 auto mechanics at a new car dealership. Greg and four other mechanics were assigned to the auto tune-up section, while the rest were assigned to other areas of the service department. During a morning break period, several mechanics from the other areas of the service department were talking with three of the auto tune-up mechanics. They were making jokes about some mistakes Greg had made. Greg was not present, so the three auto tune-up mechanics began to defend him. They said that Greg was a good employee who tried hard. Even though the three auto tune-up mechanics knew that Greg's mistakes were inexcusable, they would not participate in making jokes about Greg's lack of ability. Back in the tune-up area, they might tease Greg personally about his mistakes, but the teasing stayed within this work group.

Work groups are especially protective when the group as a whole is threatened by an outsider. This behavior is often seen when a new supervisor is placed in charge of a work group. If the new supervisor tries to make changes in procedures or work assignments too quickly, the work group joins together to fight the changes. This behavior may not be right, but it usually happens. Under such conditions any personal differences that might exist between members of the work group are quickly forgotten. The group stands together to protect itself.

COMMUNICATION AND THE GRAPEVINE

Unofficial messages passed among fellow employees are sometimes referred to as **grapevine communication**. In many businesses the grapevine tends to have a bad reputation. Employees believe that the grapevine is a system for spreading gossip and rumor. This is only partially true. The grapevine also carries good news and factual information that helps both employees and employers.

How Information Passes on the Grapevine

Special studies of grapevine communication suggest four general patterns, or chains, of communication.[1] These communication chains are presented in Illustration 5-9 and may be explained as follows:

1. The **single strand chain**. A tells B, who tells C, and so on. When we think of the grapevine, this is the common chain we picture in our minds. This chain creates the most distorted information. When A

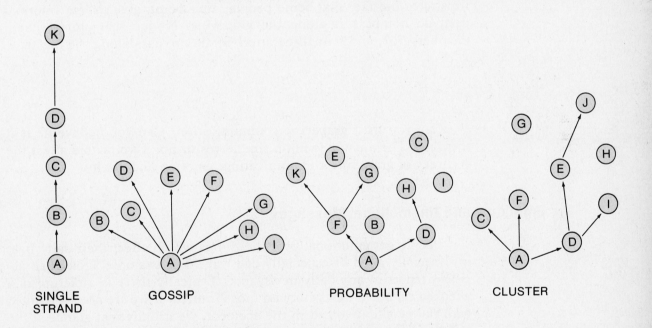

SINGLE STRAND   GOSSIP   PROBABILITY   CLUSTER

ILLUS. 5-9 Grapevine communication chains

[1]Adapted from Keith Davis, "Management Communication and the Grapevine," *Harvard Business Review*, September–October 1953, Copyright © 1953 by the President and Fellows of Harvard College; all rights reserved. p. 45.

tells B, the message is reasonably accurate. By the time the message reaches K, it is often completely different.

2. The **gossip chain**. A seeks and tells everyone else. While this pattern occurs sometimes, it is unlikely that no one else besides A would pass on the message. The gossip chain is more theoretical than real.

3. The **probability chain**. A communicates by pure chance with F and D. Then F and D communicate with whomever happens to be around them. This pattern is common for spreading gossip or rumors. It illustrates how we pass on messages in general conversation with whomever we happen to talk.

4. The **cluster chain**. A tells three selected fellow employees; perhaps one of them tells two others; and then perhaps one of them tells still another person. The cluster chain is the most common grapevine pattern. It is found in almost all organizations.

The cluster chain contains two ingredients that the other chains omit. First, it illustrates the process of selection. Many people may have information about something, but they do not tell everyone. We have a natural tendency to tell only our friends or certain people whom we think will be interested in the message. Second, the cluster chain illustrates the fact that some people, after being given some information, do not pass it along the grapevine. Notice that cluster chain members F, I, and J in Illustration 5-9 do not pass along the message.

Trusting Grapevine Communication

Can you trust grapevine communication? Can you believe it? Is it accurate? The answer is not a simple yes or no. Two factors affect the accuracy of grapevine communication: emotion and clarity.

Emotional and Unemotional Messages

People get emotional over the things which affect their daily lives in especially good or especially bad ways. For example, look at an accident report in any daily newspaper. Typically there is a picture of a wrecked car and a news story on those injured. If we are not acquainted with the people involved in the accident, we usually just glance at the story and forget it. Our reaction to the accident is *unemotional*. If we know the people or at least one person involved in the accident, we become more interested. If those injured are our friends, we have an *emotional* reaction to the bad news.

Similar emotional reactions occur when we hear good news. If a contest winner is featured in the paper, we may read it and then forget it. If our own picture is in the paper, for some reason we get excited about it. We may even cut the picture from the paper and keep it.

ILLUS. 5-10

At work, people get emotional when they think something good or bad is going to happen to them or their friends. If a good or bad situation will not affect us or our friends, we react without emotion.

The problem is that emotion distorts communication and may cause false rumors. Here is a story which shows how false rumors can get started when people get emotionally involved in a situation. A recent coal mining strike affected almost everyone in a small town near the mine. On the second day of the strike, some miners tried to cross the picket line set up by the striking miners. A small shoving match took place, but the local police stopped it almost immediately.

Back in town at the local cafe, some miners were talking about the trouble at the mine:

"Did you hear about the two brothers trying to cross the picket line?"
"Yes, the police had to break it up!"

Then later in the day at the post office, these statements from miners were heard:

"Say, I heard the police had to break up a big fight at the mine!"
"Yes, I heard the Jones brothers were arrested but the troublemakers got away."
"I heard they are coming back tomorrow with guns!"

ILLUS. 5-11

The next day only the striking miners were at the mine. Soon after, the strike was settled and everyone was back at work.

Another story will show how employees involved in a situation react emotionally and distort the communication while the unaffected employees react unemotionally and pass the message accurately. The Quik Vacuum Cleaner factory planned to expand operations and hire additional employees for two eight-hour work shifts. Somehow a rumor to the contrary was started. It was rumored that production was being cut back because of low sales and that recently hired employees were to be laid off. Below are some messages that were exchanged among senior employees and the newer employees. Notice that the senior employees react unemotionally.

Senior employee #1: I hear that they're going to lay off some of the newer employees.

Newer employee #1: Oh, I didn't hear that!

*****

Newer employee #1: Say, I understand that they are going to lay off a bunch of us.

Newer employee #2: Oh. I wonder who'll go first!

*****

Newer employee #2: Did you hear that all of the employees with less than two years' experience are being layed off?

Senior employee #2: No, I didn't. That's too bad. There must be about 25 of you.

Newer employee #2: Right!

*****

Senior employee #2: I hear that they are going to lay off about 25 of the new employees.

Newer employee #3: Oh, no!

*****

Newer employee #3: (To Newer employee #4) Did you hear about it? All of the employees who have been here less than five years are being laid off!

The point of the story above is that grapevine messages which cause employees to react emotionally are often inaccurate. The message may not be totally wrong, but most likely it will be at least partially distorted.

Clear and Unclear Messages

The second factor which determines the accuracy of the grapevine is the amount of clarity in its message. If a message is clear, the chances of distortion or improper interpretation are small. However, if a message is not clear, chances are that it will not be interpreted correctly.

For example, a grapevine message was spreading among fellow employees that the boss's son was marrying Jenny, the company mail clerk. The message was fairly accurate as to the date and place of the wedding. The problem was that Jenny Mazinger, the mail clerk, was not marrying him. The bride-to-be was Jenny Mae Singer, who worked at a company-owned factory in a different town.

ILLUS. 5-12

Unclear, or fuzzy, messages are easily distorted. If we add the emotional element to a fuzzy message, a rumor will probably develop. It is possible to improve the accuracy of your communication with fellow employees by understanding the limits of the grapevine. Most grapevine messages will contain some truth and some fuzzy distortions. Unfortunately we have no clear-cut way to determine which parts of a message are distorted. The best strategy is to recognize that the grapevine message is probably a combination of accurate and less-than-accurate information.

33 CLASS ACTIVITIES
Instant Replay

Write a short answer to each of the questions below. As you replay the answers in class, remember that you are getting feedback on your understanding of the chapter.

Questions

1. What is the meaning of horizontal communication?

   _____

   _____

2. Why is it important to try to keep communication outside the department at the horizontal level?

   _____

   _____

   _____

3. What is management's general attitude toward communication among employees? Why does management have this attitude?

   _____

   _____

   _____

   _____

4. List three concerns of a new employee at a new job.

   _____

   _____

   _____

5. When a new employee is initially accepted by a group, what three things happen?

_____

_____

_____

6. Why is communication the key to an employee's acceptance by a work group?

_____

_____

_____

7. What is the meaning of "group standards"?

_____

_____

8. What are the three general types of group standards? Give an example of each type.

_____

_____

_____

9. How does a new employee learn group standards?

_____

_____

_____

10. Give an example of what happens when an employee breaks a group standard.

_____

_____

11. What are the four areas of behavior that most work groups use to determine inclusion of a new member?

_____

_____

12. Why do most employees honor the status system of work groups?

_____

_____

13. Describe three types of informal leaders.

_____

_____

_____

14. What steps should a new employee take to become an informal leader?

_____

_____

_____

15. What is meant by "status symbols"?

_____

_____

16. Give three examples of status symbols in the world of work.

_____

_____

_____

17. Give three examples of status symbols of students at your school.

_____

_____

_____

18. How does the status of informal leaders help communication at work?

_____

_____

19. When does status become a barrier to communication? Give two examples.

_____

_____

_____

20. List two reasons why work groups stick together.

_____

_____

21. Give an example of how one communicates group cooperation.

_____

22. Give an example of how one communicates group protection.

_____

23. What is the grapevine?

_____

_____

24. What are the four types of grapevine communication chains? Which is the most common type?

_____

_____

_____

25. Describe how emotional and unemotional messages affect grapevine communication.

_____

_____

_____

26. What rumor have you heard recently? Was the rumor accurate? If so, why? If not so, why not?

_____

_____

_____

_____

Stop Talking and Look Busy!

The purpose of this activity is to aid you in understanding why some business organizations have "no talking while working" policies. The activity requires two volunteers to act, or "role-play," the situation described below. Acting ability is not important. The class will help the two role players develop their roles. At the end of the role-playing, write your answers to the questions on page 170.

Role-Playing Situation

Joe, a 22-year old cabinetmaker, works at the Stewart Wood Shop. The shop employs about 20 cabinetmakers. Each cabinetmaker works at a bench furnished by the company. The cabinetmakers supply their own tools although special tools provided by the company may be checked out from a toolroom.

Ken Green is the shop supervisor. He schedules work, keeps time records, and supervises the employees. Stated bluntly, the company policy is: "Stay at your own bench and do your own work. If you have a question, ask Mr. Green."

Mr. Green spotted Joe talking to another employee. Mr. Green was upset because he had warned Joe about talking yesterday. He watched for about five minutes; then he called Joe into his office.

Directions: The student playing the part of Mr. Green should step out of the room first. Then the class helps the student playing Joe develop his role. After this, "Joe" leaves the room to think about his role.

My suggestions for "Joe" _____

_____

_____

"Mr. Green" returns to the room, and the class helps him develop his role.

My suggestions for "Mr. Green" _____

_____

_____

"Joe" returns to the room, which is now "Mr. Green's" office. The two role players act out a discussion, reacting to each other's remarks. (Time: about five minutes)

Questions

1. Might this situation actually occur?

   _____

2. How did "Joe" and "Mr. Green" feel during their discussion?

   _____

   _____

3. What clues indicated how the role players felt?

   _____

   _____

   _____

4. How did the situation turn out?

   _____

   _____

   _____

5. What other things could "Mr. Green" have said to "Joe"? (Note any criticism you might have that what actually took place was unfair to the role players.)

   _____

   _____

   _____

6. What is your opinion of "no talking" policies at work?

   _____

   _____

7. Give additional reasons why businesses have "no talking" policies.

   _____

   _____

   _____

Case Problem: Get the Rookie

Read the case problem below carefully. As you read it, underline what you believe are key points in the case. These key points should relate to the part of the chapter dealing with joining a work group. Then answer the questions that follow.

Don Wilson, a 19-year old high school graduate, sat slumped over a cold cup of coffee in a small dirty cafe just outside of an auto assembly plant. His first day at work at the plant had started great, but that is all he cares to remember. The rest of that first day had been rough. His fellow employees put him on Assembly Point 3, the most difficult spot on that section of the line. Assembly Point 3 required four different jobs, while the other assembly points required only one or two jobs. He continually pulled the "stop line" lever because he could not keep up. Each time he stopped the line, his fellow employees laughed and the crew boss "chewed him out."

All morning long the other employees made jokes about Don's efforts. They even nicknamed him "Speedy Wilson." At lunch Don sat by himself, while the other employees played cards and talked. Don's afternoon was no better. By 3:30 p.m. he was so mad at the crew boss and the other employees that he stomped out of the plant when the quitting bell rang.

As Don left the plant, the head supervisor who had hired him asked about his day. Don bitterly told the supervisor about his painful experience, saying, "I'm surely not looking forward to tomorrow." As he sat in the cafe, he thought to himself: "I really wanted this job, but now I'm not so sure. Those guys treated me about as badly as I've ever been treated."

Questions

1. What is the issue, or problem, in this case?

_____

_____

_____

2. What is Don's relationship to the group? To the crew boss? To the supervisor?

_____

_____

3. Why did the employees and crew boss behave in the manner they did?

4. What did Don do to receive such treatment from them?

5. How does Don feel? Was he justified in complaining to the head supervisor?

6. When Don returns to work tomorrow, what are his choices in behavior toward the group?

7. What are the consequences of each alternative behavior that you listed in answer to Question 6?

8. What would you do if you were in Don's situation?

9. What similar situations have you encountered at work or at school?

10. Why is the case problem titled "Get the Rookie"?

The Hi-Hi Experiment

When we meet a friend, a relative, a teacher, a supervisor, or any-one we know, we normally greet that person by saying "Hi," "Hello," "Howdy," or "Hi, how are you?" Typically the other person responds with "Fine, how are you?" Thus, hi-hi is a ritual. It is called a ritual because we do it very often and we don't think about it very much.

This activity is an experiment to be conducted outside of your class. During the next day or so, when someone says "Hi, how are you?", answer by saying something like: "Well, not so good. I have about five problems going at the same time." Make up some problems. For example, you don't have the money for a special project; you are thinking of changing jobs; your diet program doesn't seem to be effec-tive; and so forth. Whenever possible, try to catch someone walking in the opposite direction from which you are walking.

The purpose of this experiment is to watch the unsuspecting per-son react. See what happens when you answer the ritual type greeting in a *different* way. Record your observations in the spaces provided. Then answer the questions on page 174.

Observation #1 _____

_____

_____

_____

Observation #2 _____

_____

_____

_____

Observation #3 _____

_____

_____

_____

Observation #4 _____

_____

_____

_____

Questions

1. What is meaningless conversation? Give an example.

   _____

   _____

   _____

2. When joining a new work group, do you engage in meaningless conversation? Are you sure it is really meaningless? If it is meaningless, why is it important?

   _____

   _____

   _____

   _____

   _____

3. What happens when people break the hi-hi ritual and try to carry on a discussion?

   _____

   _____

   _____

   _____

4. Why did the people you contacted in the experiment react in the ways they did?

   _____

   _____

   _____

   _____

   _____

The Status of Occupations

In 1978 a study concerning the attitudes of college students toward the status, or prestige, of certain occupations was conducted at Oklahoma State University.[2] The students were asked to rank the 15 occupations, listed below in alphabetical order, according to the amount of status given each occupation by the general public.

_____ Auto mechanics

_____ College professors

_____ Executives of large corporations

_____ Judges

_____ Labor union officials

_____ Lawyers

_____ Medical doctors

_____ Ministers

_____ Police officers

_____ Politicians

_____ Psychologists

_____ TV news reporters

_____ TV repair technicians

_____ U.S. Army generals

_____ Used car salespeople

---

[2]The study was a partial replication of the original work conducted at the University of Connecticut.

Directions

1. Working by yourself, rank each of the 15 occupations listed on page 175. Assign number one (1) to the most prestigious (high ranking) job, number two (2) to the second most prestigious job, and so on to number fifteen (15), which is the least prestigious job. Try to match the actual rank assigned to these occupations by the college students in the study mentioned earlier (which your teacher will give you later).

2. Form small groups (about five in a group). Work together to rank the 15 occupations. Try to get complete agreement through a good discussion. As much as possible, avoid "majority rules" or "horse trading." Simply because three of five people in a group agree does not mean that their answer is best. Listen to the reasons that others give for their ranking.

3. Complete the scoring worksheet on page 177. In the proper columns, record your own ranking and your group's ranking for each occupation. Then, as your teacher reads the actual rank resulting from the study mentioned, fill in that column. Now you are ready to score.

A sample scoring is given below. The sample shows that the "actual rank" for the auto mechanic is 5 and that the group rank is 7. The difference between 7 and 5, 2, is then recorded. Since "Your Rank" is 4, the difference between the actual rank, 5, and your rank, 4, is 1. A lower difference means a better score. If the small group discussion was of good quality, the group score should be closer to the actual score. This is usually true because the combined thinking of several people is usually better than the thinking of just one person alone.

Sample Score

Actual Rank	Group Rank	Your Rank	Differences Group	Differences Your	Occupation
5	7	4	2	1	Auto mechanics
6	3	2	3	4	College professors
10	8	15	2	5	Used car salespeople
TOTAL OF DIFFERENCES			7	10	

4. Answer the questions below and on pages 177–179.

Questions

1. What is the definition of "status"?

_____

_____

2. List four reasons why some jobs have higher status than others.

_____

_____

Name _____ Date _____

Scoring Worksheet

Actual Rank	Group Rank	Your Rank	Differences Group	Differences Your	Occupation
_____	_____	_____	_____	_____	Auto mechanics
_____	_____	_____	_____	_____	College professors
_____	_____	_____	_____	_____	Executives of large corporations
_____	_____	_____	_____	_____	Judges
_____	_____	_____	_____	_____	Labor union officials
_____	_____	_____	_____	_____	Lawyers
_____	_____	_____	_____	_____	Medical doctors
_____	_____	_____	_____	_____	Ministers
_____	_____	_____	_____	_____	Police officers
_____	_____	_____	_____	_____	Politicians
_____	_____	_____	_____	_____	Psychologists
_____	_____	_____	_____	_____	TV news reporters
_____	_____	_____	_____	_____	TV repair technicians
_____	_____	_____	_____	_____	U.S. Army generals
_____	_____	_____	_____	_____	Used car salespeople

TOTAL OF DIFFERENCES _____ _____

_____

_____

3. During your group discussion, what one reason was most important for ranking:

   a. TV news reporters higher or lower than politicians?

   _____

   _____

   _____

b. U.S. Army generals higher or lower than police officers?

_____

_____

_____

c. Medical doctors higher or lower than judges?

_____

_____

_____

4. Which occupation(s) gave your group the most difficulty in the ranking process? Why? How was the disagreement ended?

_____

_____

_____

_____

_____

5. What types of status symbols are associated with the following occupations?

a. U.S. Army generals _____

_____

b. Ministers _____

_____

c. Auto mechanics _____

_____

d. TV news reporters _____

_____

e. Any occupation with a status symbol that you know of which has not been mentioned in this activity.

_____

_____

6. How does a person get status?

_____

_____

_____

7. In what ways can status become a barrier to communication regardless of the occupation?

_____

_____

_____

FIRO-B³

FIRO-B is a questionnaire designed to increase your awareness of your behavior with others. It is NOT a test. The best answer is your honest opinion of yourself. The results of the questionnaire will help you find out how to improve relationships with your fellow employees. After completing and scoring the questionnaire, answer the questions on pages 184–185. These questions are a guide to the types of communication needed to improve relationships with fellow employees.

Directions: For each of the following statements (Items 1 through 16), decide which of the listed six answers best applies to you. Place the number of the answer in the blank at the left of the statement. Please be as honest as you can.

1. usually   4. occasionally
2. often   5. rarely
3. sometimes   6. never

_____ 1. I try to be with people.

³"FIRO-B, The Fundamental Interpersonal Relations Orientation-Behavior," appears in *FIRO: A Three-Dimensional Theory of Interpersonal Behavior* by William C. Schutz. Copyright © 1958 by William C. Schutz. Reprinted by permission of Holt, Rinehart and Winston and William C. Schutz.

_____ **2.** I let other people decide what to do.

_____ **3.** I join social groups.

_____ **4.** I try to have close relationships with people.

_____ **5.** I tend to join social organizations when I have an opportunity.

_____ **6.** I let other people strongly influence my actions.

_____ **7.** I try to be included in informal social activities.

_____ **8.** I try to have close, personal relationships with people.

_____ **9.** I try to include other people in my plans.

_____ **10.** I let other people control my actions.

_____ **11.** I try to have people around me.

_____ **12.** I try to get close and personal with people.

_____ **13.** When people are doing things together, I tend to join them.

_____ **14.** I am easily led by people.

_____ **15.** I try to avoid being alone.

_____ **16.** I try to participate in group activities.

Directions: For each of the next group of statements (Items 17 through 27), choose one of the following six answers:

1. most people   **4.** a few people
2. many people   **5.** one or two people
3. some people   **6.** nobody

_____ **17.** I try to be friendly to people.

_____ **18.** I let other people decide what to do.

_____ **19.** My personal relations with people are cool and distant.

_____ **20.** I let other people take charge of things.

_____ **21.** I try to have close relationships with people.

_____ **22.** I let other people strongly influence my actions.

_____ **23.** I try to get close and personal with people.

_____ **24.** I let other people control my actions.

_____ **25.** I act cool and distant with people.

_____ **26.** I am easily led by people.

_____ **27.** I try to have close, personal relationships with people.

Directions: For each of the next group of statements (Items 28 through 40), choose one of the following six answers:

1. most people   **4.** a few people
2. many people   **5.** one or two people
3. some people   **6.** nobody

_____ **28.** I like people to invite me to things.

_____ **29.** I like people to act close and personal with me.

_____ **30.** I try to influence strongly other people's actions.

_____ **31.** I like people to invite me to join in their activities.

_____ **32.** I like people to act close toward me.

_____ **33.** I try to take charge of things when I am with people.

_____ **34.** I like people to include me in their activities.

_____ **35.** I like people to act cool and distant toward me.

_____ **36.** I try to have other people do things the way I want them done.

_____ **37.** I like people to ask me to participate in their discussions.

_____ **38.** I like people to act friendly toward me.

_____ **39.** I like people to invite me to participate in their activities.

_____ **40.** I like people to act distant toward me.

Directions: For each of the next group of statements (Items 41 through 54), choose one of the following six answers:

1. usually   **4.** occasionally
2. often   **5.** rarely
3. sometimes   **6.** never

_____ **41.** I try to be the dominant person when I am with people.

_____ **42.** I like people to invite me to things.

_____ 43. I like people to act close toward me.

_____ 44. I try to have other people do things I want done.

_____ 45. I like people to invite me to join their activities.

_____ 46. I like people to act cool and distant toward me.

_____ 47. I try to influence strongly other people's actions.

_____ 48. I like people to include me in their activities.

_____ 49. I like people to act close and personal with me.

_____ 50. I try to take charge of things when I'm with people.

_____ 51. I like people to invite me to participate in their activities.

_____ 52. I like people to act distant toward me.

_____ 53. I try to have other people do things the way I want them done.

_____ 54. I take charge of things when I'm with people.

Directions for Scoring

The score sheet on page 183 shows six different areas for scoring: Expressed Inclusion, Expressed Control, Expressed Affection, Wanted Inclusion, Wanted Control, and Wanted Affection. Your scores depend upon the particular number you placed beside each statement. If the number you placed beside a statement matches any of the numbers in the "Answer" column of the score sheet, place a check mark (√) beside your answer.

Sample Score

___3___ 1. I try to be with people.

___1___ 2. I let other people decide what to do.

___5___ 3. I join social groups.

The sample items above would be scored against the score sheet on page 183 as follows:

Item 1 is found in the "Expressed Inclusion" column. Place a check mark by your answer on the questionnaire because you have a "hit." On item 1, a "hit" is a 1 or 2 or 3.

Item 2 is found in the "Wanted Control" column. Again place a check mark by your answer on the questionnaire because a "hit" on item 2 is a 1 or 2 or 3 or 4.

Item 3 is found in the "Expressed Inclusion" column. DO NOT place a check mark by your answer on the questionnaire because a "hit" on item 3 is a 1, 2, 3, or 4. The sample score for item 3 shows a 5.

Your answers may not match all of the answers on the score sheet. In some areas your "Total checked" score may be zero. In other areas, it may be 9, the maximum number of items to be checked for each area. Neither zero nor 9 is the worst or the best score.

Interpretation of the FIRO-B Scores

The general meaning of each area for scoring is presented below.

Expressed Inclusion (EI):	I join others. I include others.
Wanted Inclusion (WI):	I want people to include me.
Expressed Control (EC):	I take charge. I influence people.
Wanted Control (WC):	I want people to lead me.
Expressed Affection (EA):	I get close to people.
Wanted Affection (WA):	I want people to get close to me.

Score Sheet

Expressed Inclusion		Expressed Control		Expressed Affection	
Item	Answer	Item	Answer	Item	Answer
1	1-2-3	30	1-2-3	4	1-2
3	1-2-3-4	33	1-2-3	8	1-2
5	1-2-3-4	36	1-2	12	1
7	1-2-3	41	1-2-3-4	17	1-2
9	1-2	44	1-2-3	19	6-5-4
11	1-2	47	1-2-3	21	1-2
13	1-2	50	1-2	23	1-2
15	1	53	1-2	25	6-5-4
16	1	54	1-2	27	1-2
Total checked _____ EI		Total checked _____ EC		Total checked _____ EA	

Wanted Inclusion		Wanted Control		Wanted Affection	
Item	Answer	Item	Answer	Item	Answer
28	1-2	2	1-2-3-4	29	1-2
31	1-2	6	1-2-3-4	32	1-2
34	1-2	10	1-2-3	35	6-5
37	1	14	1-2-3	38	1-2
39	1	18	1-2-3	40	6-5
42	1-2	20	1-2-3	43	1
45	1-2	22	1-2-3-4	46	6-5
48	1-2	24	1-2-3	49	1-2
51	1-2	26	1-2-3	52	6-5
Total checked _____ WI		Total checked _____ WC		Total checked _____ WA	

Inclusion, control, and affection may also be explained by the following example: A group of people went for a car ride. Inclusion is illustrated by who went along. Control is illustrated by who is driving (or who tells the driver how to drive). And affection is illustrated by how close to each other the people are sitting.

The box below contains average scores for each of the six areas. (These average scores were given to the authors of this text-workbook during a FIRO seminar in 1977.) Write your total scores beside the average scores in the box.

	Inclusion	**Control**	**Affection**
Expressed	I join others; I include others. Average 4-7 _____	I take charge. I influence people. Average 2-5 _____	I get close to people. Average 3-6 _____
Wanted	I want other people to include me. Average 5-8 _____	I want people to lead me. Average 3-6 _____	I want people to get close to me. Average 3-6 _____

Questions

1. Within a work group, how do people

   a. communicate inclusion?

   _____

   _____

   b. communicate affection?

   _____

   _____

   c. communicate control? (Hint: status, informal leaders)

   _____

   _____

2. When a person wants to be included in a work group, how should the want be communicated?

_____

_____

_____

_____

3. When a person wants to communicate affection for a work group, how should the person do it?

_____

_____

_____

_____

4. Is it true that to get affection you must generally give affection? What problems does a person face who is high in wanting but low in expressing (a) inclusion, and (b) affection?

_____

_____

_____

_____

_____

_____

5. What steps can a person take to (a) be included in a work group, and (b) include others in a work group?

_____

_____

_____

_____

_____

_____

CHAPTER 6

Communication in Action

You are nearing the end of your study of communicating at work. During your study of this book, you have learned many facts and principles that apply to communicating in various ways with others at

ILLUS. 6-1

work. This final brief chapter is devoted to the application of those facts and principles to communication situations and problems. The problems and situations are presented within interesting and realistic case problems. Read the case problems, and then apply what you have learned about communicating at work to your reactions and solutions to the problems.

This chapter will help you put communication theory into practice. After you have read the case problems, answered the questions, and completed the activities at the end of the chapter, you should:

- Understand more about how to communicate *to* an employer.
- Be able to successfully receive and react to communications *from* employers.
- Know how to successfully determine customers' needs by communicating with them.
- Be skillful in communicating with your fellow employees.

CASE PROBLEM 1: A POOR HARVEST

ILLUS. 6-2

Harvest Time is a store devoted to the promotion and sale of food products that are healthful, nutritious, and natural. It is located in the downtown area of a city of about 200,000 people. The store has been open for about three years. Its present owner-manager is Jill, who bought the store from its previous owner about a year ago. She has three employees who perform various duties around the store such as cash register operation, produce trimming and display, ordering, customer service, and so on. Their names are Barbara, Paul, and Oscar. These three employees have worked at Harvest Time for three years.

In terms of growth and profits, Harvest Time's first two years were very successful. During this past year, however, things haven't been going very well at Harvest Time.

ILLUS. 6-3

Harvest Time financial performance charts

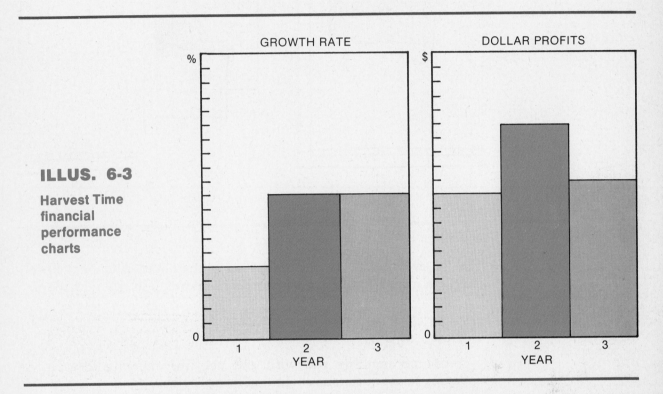

In addition to the problem of reduced growth and profits, there has recently been a lot of bickering, bad feeling, and generally low morale around Harvest Time. This situation seemed to grow with the arrival of Jill as the new owner-manager.

Jill has tried hard to establish a good communication system within the store. She has started having monthly store meetings for problem-solving, but getting people to talk at these meetings is like pulling teeth! She has installed a suggestion box, but it is always empty. She tries to talk with each employee every day, even if it is only to discuss the weather. But the employees seem embarrassed to be seen talking with her. She has even had the door removed from her office to encourage her employees to come in and see her, but nobody ever comes in for either business or personal chats. None of Jill's efforts has seemed to solve what she sees as a serious communication problem within the store.

To make matters worse, inventory and progress reports aren't getting completed. Customers are complaining about the stale merchandise. Shelves aren't getting stocked. Cash register errors are appearing.

ILLUS. 6-4

Jill's office with no door

Finally, even the floors aren't as clean as they used to be, and a problem with mice and insects is beginning to develop in the back room.

Questions

Assume anything you wish and use free-wheeling ideas in responding to the questions about this case problem.

1. What do you think is the basic problem at Harvest Time?

   _____

   _____

   _____

   _____

2. What do you suppose are the barriers to good upward communication at the store?

   _____

   _____

   _____

   _____

3. Why do you think the store meetings are so ineffective?

_____

_____

_____

4. Why isn't the suggestion box used?

_____

_____

(Is your answer to Question 4 similar to your answer to Question 3?)

5. Do you think any of the employees are negative thinkers? Why?

_____

_____

_____

6. What information is being concealed from Jill?

_____

_____

7. What advice would you give to Jill to help her solve the problem of poor communication at Harvest Time?

_____

_____

_____

_____

CASE PROBLEM 2: INSURING SUCCESSFUL DOWNWARD COMMUNICATIONS

Armelda has just been given the job of office manager at All Risk, a medium-sized insurance agency. This agency sells almost every kind of insurance. It is old and well-established and it appears to be quite successful.

The All Risk agency can insure against almost any problem.

The office staff that Armelda is to direct consists of nine persons. There are four secretaries, one clerical assistant, one filing clerk, one receptionist, one bookkeeper, and one person in charge of all of the

Armelda's office staff at All Risk

duplicating services. Each of the office staff has a work area and access to a telephone. Most of them have worked for All Risk for several years.

The previous office manager was forced to leave suddenly because of illness. There was no time for Armelda to "learn the system" existing in All Risk's office. Everyone in the office seemed to be getting along and communicating with one another. However, there didn't seem to be much in the way of a formal downward communication system. For example, there were no stated company goals or employee performance appraisals based upon those goals. There were no written company practices and procedures, job instructions, or job descriptions. Regularly scheduled office meetings did not exist.

Armelda is wondering what she should do. On the one hand, the office seems to be running smoothly without a formal downward communication system. On the other hand, she has taken a communications course and read several books on communicating at work and feels that a formal system should probably be set up.

Questions

The questions below are designed for you to provide advice to Armelda.

1. Why do you think there is no formal downward communication system at All Risk?

    _____

    _____

    _____

    _____

2. Do you think there really is *no* downward communication system there?

    _____

    _____

    _____

3. How should Armelda begin in the development of a system?

    _____

    _____

    _____

    _____

    _____

4. Is a set of job instruction procedures necessary? If so, what type would you suggest to Armelda?

_____

_____

_____

5. Do you think Armelda should establish a set of company procedures and practices? Why?

_____

_____

_____

6. Specifically, what should Armelda do about developing a set of employee performance appraisals?

_____

_____

_____

7. How can Armelda help guard against barriers to downward communication?

_____

_____

_____

_____

8. How do you think All Risk's employees will react to Armelda's communication system?

_____

_____

_____

9. What other advice do you have for Armelda?

_____

_____

_____

_____

CASE PROBLEM 3: CUSTOMER REACTIONS TO COMMUNICATIONS

This case is about customers and communication with them. It is transcribed from a tape recording made by a roving reporter/market researcher who was trying to learn something about customer reactions to banks. Mrs. Crane, the reporter, found the elderly bank customer, Mr. Dobbs, resting on a park bench in the small town square.

ILLUS. 6-5

A good way to find out how customers feel about their treatment is to ask them

The conversation between Mrs. Crane and Mr. Dobbs went as follows:

Crane: Good morning, Mr. Dobbs. I just saw you coming out of the Western Bank. May I ask you a few questions about your opinion of the bank?

Dobbs: Surely, I've got plenty of time. Ask away!

Crane: Are you a regular customer of Western Bank?

Dobbs: Yes, I've been banking there for the last 12 years.

Crane: Where did you bank before then?

Dobbs: The Eastern Bank.

Crane: Will you tell me why you changed banks?

Dobbs: I suppose I can. Actually it's kind of a long story. You see, my parents and all of our family had been customers of Eastern Bank for years. So, when it was time for me to choose a bank, I just automatically put my money in the Eastern Bank. Eventually I had a checking account, safe-deposit box, and an auto loan with Eastern. I gave them all of my financial business.

But, frankly, they didn't seem to appreciate it. Whenever I went in there, they seemed too busy to notice me. They never told me when some bank service or policy was about to change. When they did send out information, it was hard for me to understand. When they gave me a loan, they acted like they were doing me a big favor. They seemed to be continually raising their service charges and interest rates on loans for no good reason. Finally, I got tired of the kind of treatment they were giving me. So, I took *all* of my business to the Western Bank across the street.

Crane: What has your experience been at the Western Bank?

Dobbs: Well, even though they are large, they seem to be interested in me and every other customer.

Crane: What do you mean by "interested"?

Dobbs: I don't know exactly. But they all know me and call me by name when I come into the bank. They seem willing to listen to my requests. They write letters to me, announcing in advance any changes in bank policy, services, or charges. I am able to understand such letters. They aren't snoopy, and they respect confidential information. They take time to explain things to me. To sum it up, I guess they seem genuinely interested in me.

Crane: That's all very interesting, Mr. Dobbs. Thank you very much for your time and your thoughts.

ILLUS. 6-6

Mr. Dobbs took all his financial business from the Eastern Bank to the Western Bank

Questions

Assume that you are the market researcher and that you have been employed to give advice to the management of the Eastern Bank.

1. What would you suggest to the Eastern Bank regarding written communications to customers?

_____

_____

_____

_____

2. Do you think the training of Eastern Bank employees should include anything about speaking to customers? If so, give three examples of the training you believe is necessary.

_____

_____

_____

3. Do you think Eastern Bank's employees were *listening* to Mr. Dobbs? Why or why not?

_____

_____

_____

_____

4. What barriers to communication existed between Eastern Bank and Mr. Dobbs?

_____

_____

_____

_____

5. What additional general advice about communications would you give to the people who work at Eastern Bank?

_____

_____

_____

_____

_____

CASE PROBLEM 4: CARLITA'S CONCERN

As a new summer employee of Haufield School District #107, Carlita was determined to be a good employee. She had been chosen over several other applicants. When she was hired, her supervisor told her that there had been problems during previous summers. The summer employees tended to "goof off." They spent a lot of time talking, joking, and playing. The supervisor made it clear that, if Carlita wanted to keep her job, she must work hard and be productive.

The duties of the summer employees were many and varied. They included painting classrooms and offices, cleaning, sweeping, waxing floors, and dusting furniture. On some days their duties involved cutting grass, repairing fences, and tending flower beds. The summer employees also did repair work on playground equipment.

On her first day at work, Carlita wanted to make a good impression on her fellow employees. She was also committed to working hard to please her employer. But what she saw that day posed a great dilemma!

ILLUS. 6-7

The summer employees were apparently more committed to having fun than to working. They were supposed to be weeding the flower beds, but two people were playing "catch." Another had a blaring portable radio. Still another was slowly picking dandelions for a bouquet. But whenever they spotted the supervisor driving up, they all acted very busy weeding the flower beds. Their "work behavior" could be summed up as "When the cat is away, the mice will play."

Questions

Obviously Carlita has a problem. She wants to do her job well, but she also wants to be accepted as a part of the summer crew. Assume that the members of the summer crew will probably *not* be fired. Help solve Carlita's problem by answering the questions below.

1. What are some of the general standards of the work group?

_____

_____

_____

_____

2. How are those general standards being communicated to Carlita?

_____

_____

_____

_____

3. How should Carlita determine the social standards of the group?

_____

_____

_____

_____

4. The group's production standards seem to be giving Carlita the greatest amount of immediate concern. How can she reconcile her (higher) standards with the group's (lower) standards?

_____

_____

_____

_____

5. What might be involved in an "inclusion test" for Carlita?

_____

6. Do you think she should try to pass the inclusion test? Why?

7. What would be a good communications strategy that would help Carlita become a member of the work group *and* please her employer too?

You have now reached the end of the first part of your study of communicating at work. You have learned why communication is important and how to communicate with employers, customers, and fellow employees. In this chapter you have had some realistic practice through cases in solving communication problems at work. After you have completed the activities at the end of this chapter, the next part of your study is to go out and practice better communication with others at work, at school, and at play.

CLASS ACTIVITIES
Instant Replay

This final "instant replay" is designed to help you remember the basic communication principle involved in each of the four case problems in Chapter 6.

Questions

1. If you could suggest only one thing to Jill at Harvest Time that would help improve upward communication in the store, what would it be?

   _____

   _____

   _____

2. Comment on the following statement: "It is possible for an excellent and effective informal communication system to exist in a business."

   _____

   _____

   _____

3. Why do you think it is so important for a bank to have a good strategy for communicating with its customers?

   _____

   _____

   _____

4. What might happen if Carlita ignores the work group's behavior and simply works hard to meet her own standards?

   _____

   _____

   _____

Communication Crossword

The crossword puzzle on page 203 should be a fun activity for you to complete. It draws upon information from all of the six chapters in this text.

Across

2. Term describing a message from employee to employer
3. Term describing a manager's message to an employee that a job is well done
6. The art of sending or receiving business messages that are understood
7. Something we believe is true but cannot prove with facts
9. The test a new employee must meet to be accepted by most work groups
11. One of the most poorly developed communication skills
12. One of the first communication skills human beings learn
14. Term describing a message from a superior to a subordinate

Down

1. May sometimes be used to spread official business messages
4. May sometimes be distorted to hide negative feelings
5. Level of communication among fellow employees
6. Something to be overcome to achieve effective communication
8. Too many of these form a barrier to downward communication
10. Anyone who buys a product or a service
13. Example of a barrier to effective communication with customers
15. Communication symbols which are a very important part of our lives

Name _____ Date _____

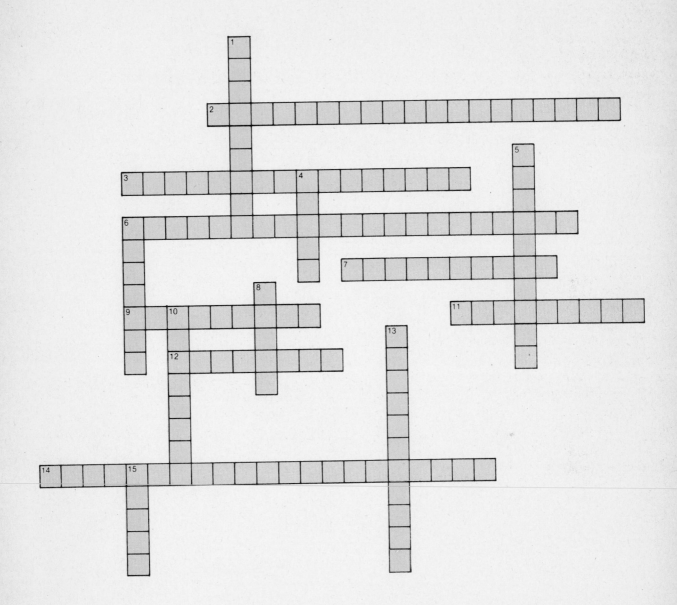

Your Progress Record

This activity will help you measure the progress you have made in developing communication skills as a result of reading this book and completing all the activities.

Situations That I Have Faced	How I Handled the Situation Before Reading This Book	My Plans for Handling the Situation in the Future
Receiving negative feedback		
Working closely with a negative thinker		
Feeling defensive after making an error		
Noticing a sad look on a friend's face		
Listening to job instructions		
Feeling afraid to tell the boss unpleasant news		
Daydreaming and private planning		

Index

and the open manager, 83–84
barriers and gateways to, 78–86
definition of, 67–70
effective and ineffective forms of, 70
methods of, 68–69
types of, 70–74

E

effects of status on communication:
    clarifies some questions, 153–154
    constitutes a barrier to effective communication, 155–156
    facilitates communication, 154–155
employers:
    communicating to, 31–54
    communication from, 67–86

F

facts and judgments, differences between, 77–78
fear (as a barrier to effective upward communication):
    of being labeled as emotional, 44–45
    of being penalized, 42–43
    of embarrassment, 43–44
    of the manager, overcoming, 48–50
    recognizing the barrier of, 49–50
    taking action to eliminate, 50
feedback:
    getting immediate, 80–82
    negative, 6–7, 75–78
    positive, 4–6
    providing, 4–7
feelings:
    about the business, 38–39
    about the manager, 39
    about work, 39
    their need to be communicated upward, 39
fellow employees, communicating with, 139–164

G

gossip chain, 160
grapevine communication:
    cluster chain, 160
    defined, 159
    gossip chain, 160
    probability chain, 160
    single strand chain, 159
    trusting, 160–162

grapevine, how information passes on the, 159–160
group acceptance, initial, 143–144
group standards, types of:
    general, 145–147
    production, 148–149
    social, 147–148

H

horizontal communication:
    definition of, 139–142
    management's attitude toward, 142
    outside departments, 140–142
    within departments, 140

I

inclusion test, the, 149–150
informal group leaders, status of, 151–153
information overload:
    as a barrier to upward communication, 45–47
    defined, 45
    overcoming the barrier of, 51–53
    recognizing, 51–52
    taking action to conquer, 52–53

J

job instructions, defined, 70
job rationale, defined, 70
joining a work group:
    group standards, 145–148
    inclusion test, the, 149–150
    initial group acceptance, 143–144

L

listening (as a communication skill), 14–16
listening to customers, 117–120

M

managers:
    closed, 82
    closed and open, comparison of, 83
    fear of, 39–45
    open, 83
matters of fact, 75–76

effective, barriers to, 38–48
effective, overcoming barriers to, 48–54
purpose of, 32–34
types of, 34–38

W

wage-and-benefits leader, 152
work group behavior, communication and, 143

work groups:
   joining, 143–150
   status in, 150–157
   sticking together of, 157–158
writing (as a communication skill), 16–17
written forms of communication to customers:
   advertisements, 107
   business letters, 105–107
   hints for improving, 107